This Hungry Spirit

This Hungry Spirit

Your Need for Basic Goodness

C. Clinton Sidle

Larson Publications

Burdett, New York

Library of Congress Control Number: 2009931853

Publisher's Cataloging-In-Publication Data
(Prepared by The Donohue Group, Inc.)

Sidle, C. Clinton.
    This hungry spirit : your need for basic goodness / C. Clinton Sidle.

    p. : ill. ; cm.

    Includes bibliographical references and index.
    ISBN: 978-1-936012-45-9

1. Self-realization. 2. Self-realization--Anecdotes. 3. Self-realization--
Problems, exercises, etc. 4. Happiness. 5. Conduct of life. I. Title.

BF637.S4 S53 2009
158   2009931853

Published by Larson Publications
4936 NYS Route 414
Burdett, New York 14818 USA

Permissions

The author and publisher gratefully acknowledge the following sources for permission to reproduce material under copyright:

    Poem, page 11: "Self Portrait," from page 9, *Fire in the Earth,* by David Whyte, copyright © 1992, reproduced by permission of Many Rivers Press

    For Exercise 22, page 89, Ken Blanchard, et. al. *Leading at a Higher Level,* (New Jersey: Financial Times Press, 2007). Susan Fowler developed this process for the Situational Self Leadership program offered by The Ken Blanchard Companies.
    For more information, go to www.kenblanchard.com

larsonpublications.com

18   17   16   15   14   13   12   11   10   09

10   9   8   7   6   5   4   3   2   1

FSC
Mixed Sources
Product group from well-managed
forests and other controlled sources

Cert no. SW-COC-002283
www.fsc.org
© 1996 Forest Stewardship Council

Contents

Your hungry spirit . . . Is guided by your mental models . . . Those models
are shaped by your mental chatter . . . Most of that chatter is about you
. . . But the models are not real . . . And they can cause problems

They are self-limiting

They cause stress

They make problems in relationships

They separate us from ourselves

You can change your mental models . . . Where you suffer often gives
the clue . . . Yet choosing is still difficult . . . Because you first must find
your basic goodness . . . What is this basic goodness, really? . . . When
you find it, you find not only happiness but also success

Exercises

Acknowledgements

THIS BOOK is the result of a lifelong journey of wanting to become a better person and to help create a better world. Many people have contributed to this journey as guides and teachers and this work would not have been possible without them. So I want to acknowledge them here. I have acknowledged many of them before in my previous work, and I do so again because of their importance to what they came to teach me.

Molly Elmo and Beatrice Sidle, my mother and grandmother, for having such a strong and comforting faith in me.

Harry Kisker for planting the seed as a young adult, and for being a true inspiration and a lifelong friend.

Sri S. N. Goenka for introducing me to meditation and a new view of freedom.

Paula Peter for helping to reveal the full complexity of romantic relationship and its challenging lessons.

Aubryn and Connor Sidle, my children, for opening my heart and being the special beings I had hoped them to be.

Rodney Napier for his mentorship in working with groups, and for showing me the importance of intentional design in experiential learning.

Dan Tillemans for his friendship and counsel, and for introducing me to the power of using the outdoors in my work.

Roxi Bahar Hewartson for being a loyal friend and long-term learning partner on my journey.

Chester Warzynksi for fully appreciating my journey and serving as
a constant counsel, friend, and inspiration.

Peter Hurst for his friendship and patience, and his willingness to
ask and ponder some very difficult questions.

Anne MacQuarrie for leading me to Shambhala training, the power
of basic goodness, and the teachings of Chogyam Trungpa
Rinpoche.

Chogyam Trungpa Rinpoche for his profound vision for the world
and creating enlightened society.

Khenchen Palden Sherab Rinpoche and Khenpo Tsewang Dongyal
Rinpoche for being my root teachers.

Roy H. Park, Jr., and his family for generously providing a wonderful
practice field in the form of the Roy H. Park Leadership Fellows
Program

The Park Fellows and other Cornell Johnson School business school
students for helping me to work out, internalize, and fortify the
lessons of my work.

Mary Tomaselli for being a true friend and providing a critical eye
to much of the content of this book.

Jennifer Cottrell for showing me the depth that freedom can bring
to a romatic relationship and patiently giving stylistic guidance
that I have found so essential to expressing my message.

I also want to give a special thanks to my editor and publisher Paul
Cash who has greatly enriched and brought more to life many of the
fundamental ideas herein.

INTRODUCTION
This Hungry Spirit

It doesn't interest me if there is one God
or many gods.
I want to know if you belong or feel
abandoned.
If you know despair or can see it in others.
I want to know
if you are prepared to live in the world
with its harsh need
to change you. If you can look back
with firm eyes
saying this is where I stand. I want to know
if you know
how to melt into that fierce heat of living
falling toward
the center of your longing. I want to know
if you are willing
to live, day by day, with the consequence of love
and the bitter
unwanted passion of your sure defeat.

I have been told, in *that* fierce embrace, even
the gods speak of God.

—David Whyte, "Self Portrait"
© 1992 Many Rivers Press

I KNOW THERE IS A HUNGER IN YOU, longing to be filled. Just stop and look for a moment, and you will find it. You feel it don't you? You may be successful, yet still you strive. You may be wealthy, yet still you seek gain. You may be loved, yet you still wander. Where does this discontent begin? There is always something missing. What do you so long for?

For me, it has always been freedom. A long time ago I wrote about it just before entering a difficult time in my life.

> Freedom has a new meaning for me. When I was younger it meant the freedom to travel, to pursue different relationships, and to follow my deepest yearnings. Above all it meant adventure—as in the year I studied and traveled in Europe, hitchhiking and sleeping under the stars.

> I remember one trip in particular that captured the essence of this freedom. My friend and I hitchhiked from Belgium, down the Rhine visiting castle ruins, across Bavaria to the Oktoberfest in Munich, down to Switzerland, and back up the Rhine through the Black Forest. We followed our every whim, looking for adventure and asking people on the way where they were headed and what might be interesting there for us. We slept in a pedestrian tunnel to avoid the rain and were awakened in the early morning by a tractor that nearly ran us over—the driver just shouted something in German and laughed as he drove away.

> We brawled at the Oktoberfest with some others, and I spent the night in the hospital where I had stitches for a cut from being hit over the head with a beer mug while protecting my friend during the fight. We climbed and spent the night on a Swiss mountaintop, passing farmers on the way carrying huge bales of hay on steeply sloped pastures and a hermit who was intrigued with my friend's nylon backpack. And we traveled to Freiburg in the Black Forest for a wine festival, where we spent the night in a residential downtown courtyard and found ourselves locked in overnight and forced to climb over a high wall to leave.

Never before had I had such a sense of complete freedom from responsibility, worry, or direction. For the longest time I yearned to return to that place.

As I've grown older, the meaning of freedom has changed. I still like adventure but it's no longer as compelling. Now I seek a different kind of freedom—the freedom to be vulnerable and emotionally expressive, and to be open, honest, and truthful about what I feel. Even more, I want to love easily and freely without condition or inhibition. I want to feel the pain and the joy of all of life with the greatest depth, but without attachment to the ebb and flow.

I want to be free in sensing and expressing feeling and emotion, to flow with them naturally without the suffering that comes from holding or rejecting. I want to become as one with them, because in separation I feel the tension and conflict of thinking I must do something about them. I want to be fully present with whatever arises, and flow with it freely, with full awareness, and without hesitation—that is total freedom, that is what I long for. To experience deeply the ups and downs, the love and anger, the compassion and fear of daily life, and to not judge, hold, or control.

It feels this longing for freedom is really about exploring my real self—finding the details in my daily existence that bring to life the different, and sometimes hidden, but more authentic parts of me. I have difficulty describing it because I haven't yet fully experienced it. Maybe it's a search for my soul. I'm not sure.

I'm only sure what it is not. It is not judging myself for being jealous. It is not willful behavior as when I shut everything out and focus only on the goal or idea at hand. And it is not living in the past or in the future, as when I dwell on a painful memory or a hopeful expectation. These are attachments to the known.

Freedom springs from experiencing the unknown, and that can only happen from moment to moment.

The driving force in my life has always been this longing. We all share some version of it. It is a universal aspect of our nature and it underlies all that we do. We have many different words for it—yearning, questing, searching, craving, striving, seeking, thirsting . . . to do whatever we are compelled to do. It is as gross as a drive to accomplish a big goal, and it as subtle as an uneasy restlessness.

It is a pervasive energy I call our spirit, our hungry spirit. Different people call it different things; but whatever it is, it is your constant longing for success, recognition, influence, freedom, love, or whatever it takes for you to find your place in the world. All your worldly concerns are subordinate to it and means to its end. It helps you find and make meaning, and drives you to achieve and do something with your life. It is the seed of creation and drives the pulse of your evolutionary urge. It is your life force, your life energy: Every act, every word, every thought is a reflection of it in some way.

What is this hungry spirit really looking for? Aristotle said happiness, which he considered "the meaning and purpose of life, the whole aim and end of human existence." But the trouble with calling it happiness is that in this day and age we tend to cheapen it into getting something for nothing.

Many New Age self-help and happiness programs, for instance, tell you that you can fulfill your desires by simply visualizing what you want—as if the Universe were a catalogue that you can flip through and shop with free and near-instant delivery. Sorry, it's not that simple. Worse, these promoters of happiness can misrepresent how things actually do work, and often ignore the fact that there is something very valuable to learn from another part of yourself, from your suffering and other negative feelings.

Suffering is a fundamental truth of being human, and in that suffering often lay the seeds to our growth. Many of us already know, for example, that there is something to be learned from sadness: It reconciles us to reality and awakens us to the flowing, changing nature of life.

> Most of what we take for happiness is delusional.
> •

The fact is that most of what we take for happiness is delusional. In spite of all our efforts to find it, get it, be it, we're not getting any happier, and maybe we're even getting worse.

Although our income has more than doubled over the past fifty years, research shows we have become no happier. When we reach a certain level—and that threshold isn't very high—money makes no difference. Yet still we pursue even more along with reputation, achievement, pleasure, and companionship, all in the name of happiness. It's never-ending, and when we fail to be satisfied, we are often overcome with resignation or depression. Today more than a hundred million people suffer from depression, and that number is growing. So in spite of all our pursuits, we still seem lost and confused.

The reason, I believe, is that what our hungry spirit longs for is not just about happiness. I believe it longs for what I call "meaning"—something that draws into us what matters most to us, and gives fullness to what we do and who we are. What we all really want to find is a sense of relevance, purpose, and belonging in our lives, and how well the pursuit of that goes is what gives us greater or lesser happiness. The question of "Who am I, and why am I here?" is the root to all of our pursuits, and the answer it draws can be the source of our deepest resilience.

As the old saying goes, "If you don't *stand* for anything, then you will *fall* for almost everything"; but if you know your *why,* then you can bear almost any *how.* Do materialistic pursuits and getting what you want bring lasting happiness? No, because they serve no lasting purpose and only demand you do more of the same. Your longing becomes a treadmill that just spins faster and faster and eventually begins to feel empty. No wonder we are stressed and depressed. What we typically take for happiness sells ourselves short. Like Lily Tomlin said, "The problem with the rat race is that even if you win, you're still a rat."

The real problem is that you can't possibly know what you want if you don't first know who you are. And you can't possibly know who you are unless you challenge yourself to find what is most meaningful to you. Most of us never even really look, because it requires going inward. This is not easy in our fast-paced world, and not everyone has the courage for it. But if you invest the time, I guarantee that you will gain insights into what is otherwise

> The real problem is that you can't possibly know what you want if you don't first know who you are.
> •

hidden, and slowly come to a fuller life. This takes you deeper into your own longing—well beyond shallow notions of happiness as simply getting what you think you want.

When I was a young man, a close friend shared an ancient notion that helped me frame this longing early in life. He said that in the Hindu tradition there are four phases of life, and each phase builds on the last in a progressive process that leads to finding deeper and deeper meaning as well as greater and greater happiness. I quickly adopted a version of it as a guide for my life and have since discovered a number of others in psychology and other spiritual traditions. In my version, there are just three phases:

Phase 1: Study and exploration—Acquiring the socialized self
Phase 2: Love and contribution—Discovering the authentic self
Phase 3: Spirit and devotion—Exploring the transcendent self

This book is about navigating the second, middle phase. It is about carefully unraveling the socialized, conditioned self to discover a truer or more authentic self. Your hungry spirit is constantly driving you to do and acquire things, and much of what you acquire in the first phase is a build-up of perceptions, complexes, and roles that you take on to deal with your world in becoming an adult. In the process, you very likely develop a self-image that is based on the expectations of others and the conditioning of your world. This separates you from your true self and eventually begins to cause you problems. *But it is supposed to happen this way—it's nature's big set-up to ensure you continue to grow.*

In the middle phase you unlearn a lot of that to find what is more meaningful and authentic—the real you. You dissolve the acquired in ways that help you discover the innate. In a sense, this unavoidably mysterious process *is about losing yourself in order to find yourself.* In that discovery, you begin to lose your sense of dependence on others and gain a sense of who you really are. You connect to a deeper, more authentic you, gain a deeper sense of confidence, and learn to open and extend yourself out in love and contribution.

The third phase is exploring the relationship of this authentic self to the cosmos. It is about divine love and transcending your sense of individual existence. I'll leave that part to you.

I've been a student of leadership for many years and there is one thing I know for sure: The better you know yourself and are grounded in the real, authentic you, the more likely you are to not only be happy, but also successful . . . and to want to do good in the world. When you feel good about yourself, you are more predisposed to being supportive, charitable, cooperative, and productive. So what *really* makes you happy also makes you successful.

I *could* frame this book around leadership, but I'd rather not. I would rather talk about it as human effectiveness. After all, that's what leadership is really about anyway.

Being an effective human being is less about mastering certain skills and more about fostering a certain attitude in yourself as well as in others. As management guru Peter Block says, "It is about confronting yourself and others with your own freedom." It's about learning who you really are.

In sharing with you what I have to say, I will reveal a fair amount of my personal history. I do this because there is a story to tell, and because I want to show you that this process isn't something abstract, some theory. It's a very doable and worthwhile way to live your life. Many happiness and leadership authors invent examples, use others as examples, or cite research to make their points. In contrast, I want to make this very real, practical, and convincing for you—so you'll want to try it yourself.

PART ONE

The Lesser and Greater Spirit

1

The Grip of the Lesser Spirit: How You Limit Yourself

"When we get to wishing a great deal for ourselves, whatever we get soon turns into mere limitation and exclusion."

—George Eliot

I CRUISED INTO MY THIRTIES feeling very fortunate and confident. I was a proud father of two, had a beautiful Greek revival home on a babbling brook, a marriage that many admired, a promising fast track career with great visibility, and in general, a terrific life in my prosaic hometown. There was every reason to be happy; but I often wondered whether I really was, and even suspected I was not. Something seemed missing.

I was still searching—reading the great works in world literature, religion, and philosophy while also practicing meditation. No one other than my wife, though, knew of my interest in these things at the time. I was holding part of myself back—hiding it for fear of someone taking it the wrong way.

As written in my journal entry in the introduction, I wanted to access and express a deeper part of myself; but it was still just an idea, and I wouldn't risk the vulnerability it required. That taste of freedom I'd had and still yearned for, I just put back in the box. I tried to ignore it, as if it were not important anymore. I'm not even sure I was conscious of doing that at the time. Instead, I modeled my life around what was expected, and did what I believed I should do to make my friends and family happy. It was safer that way. Besides, I actually did think that they were right, and I was wrong. How could it be otherwise? So I learned to make my way through discipline and control, and thought it was no problem to go against my grain.

Yet I gradually found myself somehow disconnected, from others and even from myself. People who knew me considered me distant, even aloof. I was bored and often dreamt of other things. I longed for something new but wouldn't share what it was with anyone, in part because I just didn't know. So instead of feeling free, I felt a prisoner of my own longing.

Then things began to fall apart. What happened?

Your hungry spirit

Before answering that directly, I want to show you a certain quality of this hungry spirit that is important to understand. I don't want to just give it to you, so please listen inside to this series of questions I adapted from a poem by Leo Buscaglia. See if you can tell what the quality is.

Have you ever not . . .
cried to not risk appearing too sentimental?
made an effort to not risk failure?
shared your feelings to not risk exposing your true self?
revealed a dream to not risk looking like a fool?
reached out to another to not risk involvement?
loved for risk of not being loved in return?

If your answer is yes to any of these questions, what is it, then, that holds you back?

> The elemental fear of being inadequate or not being enough.
>
> •

This longing, hungry spirit of yours can be tracked to something deep inside you—an elemental fear of being inadequate or not being enough. You know you have it—we all have it. Many of our world traditions talk about it: We somehow have fallen from grace, possess an Original Sin, or have obscured our true nature, leaving us feeling incomplete. To compensate, we strive to become whole, and this explains many of our motivations.

Out of this basic fear or insecurity, you try to prove to the world that you are worthy of it based on its own terms. You learn from the adults in your childhood how to become one of them, and you adopt their ways, both good and bad. You learn to achieve, to succeed, and to advance, often in the name of happiness. Yet your drives for wealth, power, and acquisition as well as for position, prestige, and recognition all stem from a desire to become greater than what you fear yourself to be. Sadly though, as you grow up, having more and consuming more does not seem to fill the void.

In trying to prove yourself, you develop a self-image that either lives out this pattern or rebels against it. Neither response is authentic. You simply define yourself to be *just like or just the opposite of* the big people in your life, and you never gain a clear sense of who you really are. Instead you accumulate habits and attitudes that mirror your upbringing and construct a socialized-for-success you that doesn't reflect your real inner truth. You then project it and act it out in scripted ways like "get a job, get married, and get a home." Or, if you rebel, you do the same with some version of "turn away, tune in, and drop out." In both cases, you do it without ever consciously questioning it.

> To compensate, you try to prove to the world that you are worthy of it based on its own terms.
> •

> You accumulate habits and attitudes that mirror your upbringing and construct a socialized-for-success you that doesn't reflect your inner truth.
> •

These scripted ways then affect your ability to be happy and successful in your career, relationships, marriage, and parenting—every aspect of your life. Eventually they cause you problems because they are not the real you. For everyone I've met wanting to succeed in the job they are doing, for instance, I have often found that same person longing for a different life or losing enthusiasm for their work. To not respond to—or worse, to not even ask about—your true calling, can suck the life out of work.

Many marriages break up from the collapse of these projections and scripted ways and those that persist in them can still be badly scarred.

We often admire long-term relationships, but we shouldn't automatically esteem a fifty-year marriage without knowing what happened to the souls of the people in it. As parents too we can project our unlived lives and ideas about ourselves onto our children. It's our way of living vicariously. This places a large burden on them by driving a wedge between who they really are and what we want them to be—between *their truth* and *our fiction*.

We have all known such families. I knew one that was headed in that direction but turned it all around quite dramatically. He was a first genera-tion American of Middle Eastern descent. She was from a family with deep roots in the Midwest. They met at the end of the Second World War and were fully in love: He had found his life's love and she her white knight. They had four children, and after a while their perfect match began to have problems.

Mirroring what they had learned growing up, he became so dictatorial that he bordered on the abusive, and she so submissive that she seemed to just disappear. There was constant stress in the family as he laid down the law and she gave in, but neither knew another way. Eventually there were problems with the children, too; and about seventeen years into the marriage their eldest daughter began to rebel. Thinking a change in scenery would help, they sent her to her mother's childhood home in the Midwest for the summer. She was arrested there for possession of drugs. That was the turning point.

Feeling that he somehow was failing his family, he began to question his motives: What was he doing wrong, and how might he change? He saw that he had been blindly following the ways he had learned from his parents, and also saw that those old ways were not working for him or his family. He needed a new way but didn't know where to start. So he simply tried to take more a genuine interest in his wife and children, and to focus more on *their* needs instead of simply getting *his* way. He became more accepting, flexible, and supportive. As he changed, his family changed; and as they felt better, he felt better. They began to heal, and their love for one another grew. She gradually blossomed into a fount of humor and wisdom for the family.

He realized that his new outlook also worked in other areas of his life—so much so that he literally became an ideal model of someone who can make a significant change, even in midlife. He became an admired leader in every aspect of his life. Instead of "my way or the highway," he learned to listen to and support the ways of others too. At work he became a successful employee advocate, in Freemasonry a servant leader, and in his small village a voice for renewal and community. They were married for more than sixty years and he grew to be widely esteemed, but even in his last years he still held remorse for the way he had been. That painful memory was a constant reminder to continue to be the person he had become.

We should all be so lucky.

What I'm describing here is the breakdown of patterns developed in the first phase of life. To choose not to awaken from that phase is almost unforgivable. Otherwise, this unconscious split between your projections and reality, and between the acquired and the innate, drives your entire experience and sense of who you are. You remain a prisoner of your childhood, no matter how successful you may appear to be in your outer life.

The most important thing to realize at this stage is that *you can ride this hungry spirit* to gain your freedom. It works on the basis of the information you selectively feed it—thoughts, beliefs, and attitudes.

As we shall see, *there is both a lesser and a greater hungry spirit*. This spirit serves you poorly when it is grounded in the lesser, in fear and insecurity, and directed towards thoughts, feelings, and activities that *defend* or *project* you. It serves you best when it is grounded in the greater, in feeling good about yourself, and directed toward things that reach beyond you.

This is how it operates.

Is guided by your mental models

I am going to say a few words—please pay attention to the image or thought that immediately comes to your mind.

Lawyer.

What visual image comes to mind? It might be a person in a suit or a courtroom. Is it? How about . . .

School.

Do you see a name or a building of one that you attended? Or . . .

Mother.

Is it your Mom, or a woman holding a baby at her breast? Or? What do you see?

These images are your mental models and your hungry spirit is guided by them.

Mental models are acquired habitual patterns of thought and feeling that guide your action and determine what you see and perceive, and they are self-reinforcing.

> Mental models are your filters and lenses through which you interpret your world.
> •

We all have them, whether we are conscious of them or not. They are your filters and lenses through which you interpret your world, and through which you project your ideas of how things should or shouldn't work. Like the film in an old movie projector, they make your reality.

We have different mental models for different situations, literally dozens of them in our lives. They are embedded in our belief systems, our culture, our language, and our personal style. They can be simple generalizations such as "accountants are number crunchers" or deeper more complex thoughts like "children should be seen and not heard." We accept and believe them so completely that we live our lives by them. We construct them out of bits and pieces through our personal histories—ideas accepted from others or repeated to our self, including notions of job, race, religion, gender—and we live them as if we are them.

Mental models are abstract simplifications of reality. They are models and frameworks, and you couldn't function without them. Some of them are important and serve you well, while others don't and cause you endless grief. If I believe people to be trustworthy, for instance, I would likely be open, make friends easily, and take more risks with relationships. On the other hand, if I believe people to be untrustworthy, I would likely have fewer intimate friends, be more closed and defended, and maybe even be a little depressed.

One of the mental models I acquired is that I view myself as independent and don't like to conform to the norms of an organization. Some might call it "a problem with authority"; but whatever it is, it is definitely the rebel mode of response to the world. A related one is that even though my co-workers don't always take me seriously because of it, I know I can "make it happen." These mental models have worked both for me and against me over the years.

Another is about my weight. I was rather chunky in grade school. After recess one day, my fifth-grade teacher was reading us a story that used a new word, "stout," so she tried to define it for us. She said, "Now take my friend Clint here, he's not fat, he's just stout." As my childhood friend said years later, "I was there the day your life changed!" I was so embarrassed that from that point forward, I was obsessed with my weight. I dieted, worked out, and weighed myself at least once a day for the next couple of decades.

We all have these things. Some of our relationship ones include "Men look only for women who are slender," or "I make most men feel intimidated," or "Men are insensitive, women are needy." Other common ones, both good and bad, are:

People are trustworthy	People are untrustworthy
I have something special to offer	I'm afraid of being just average
I can do it if I try hard enough	I don't have the experience
I think others are basically good	I think others are basically a pain
I know my priorities	I can't say no
I like to learn	I like to be right
I like to experiment	I like to look good
I do what is right	I do what I'm told
I know what I want	I can't have what want
I feel good about me	I'm not attractive
I see the good in my work	I hate my job

Try this exercise to see some of yours.

Exercise 1: Identifying your mental models

1. Think of the different aspects of your life—work, play, family, children, friends, or whatever makes sense to you. What mental models do you have? What do you tell yourself over and over in them?
2. Think of at least ten and write them down under the headings of the different aspects of your life you've chosen.
3. Which ones work *for* you?
4. Which ones work *against* you?

These models are shaped by your mental chatter

These mental models are formed and reinforced by your mental chatter. If you stop for a second, notice there is a constant chatter, an ongoing monologue, inside your mind—about work, children, friends, and so on. It's an unending, discursive stream of noise about everything in your life.

When you look more closely, you start to see that this noise has patterns. Each thought or feeling disappears but leaves an imprint on the mind and heart. That imprint gets stronger and deeper as it is repeated over and over and develops into a pattern that can become very powerful over the course of decades.

These patterns accumulate and solidify, and become your ideas, beliefs, fears, habits, and attitudes. They come from your parents, relatives, teachers, friends, and society—often via media. Most of us pick them up and absorb them without examination and they become our filters through which we experience life. As the Buddha said, "What we are today comes from our thoughts of yesterday, and our present thoughts build our life of tomorrow: Our life is a creation of the mind."

Exercise 2: Watching your mental chatter

1. Take a few minutes a day for a week, sit quietly, and pay attention to the thoughts that go through your mind.

2. Take note of what they are about and how often you think them.

3. Write them down in categories—family, work, friends, romance, sports, fashion, daydreaming, and so on.

4. Are they associated with the past, the present, the future?

5. What kinds of emotions come with them—fear, anger, love, joy...?

6. What drives them?

Most of that chatter is about you

Think about how everything you do is in some way concerned with you—competition, achievement, acquisition, growth, getting better, and so on. Health, wealth, and companionship seem to be our chief concerns. Also think about how much time you spend preoccupied with what others are thinking of you, and how you might influence their thoughts. My bet is that like most of us, you are always concerned with your self-image, and obsessed with "looking good and not looking stupid." The maintenance of your perceived self is the motive behind much of your behavior.

> My bet is that like most of us, you are always concerned with your self-image, and obsessed with "looking good and not looking stupid."
> •

In the actions that you take, for instance, are you more concerned with doing by others or looking good? Even in your more altruistic moments, with friends and family, you might still be thinking and doing for yourself. Do you support your family for its own sake, or do you do it because you believe this is what a good provider does and you want people to think well of you? Most of your thoughts and actions are somehow related to how you want the world to work for you and what you can get from it.

This grip of self-concern is your hungry spirit seeking to complete itself through the activities you undertake—*but that drive is rooted in your lesser spirit*, in the fear and insecurity we talked about before. As a result, it takes on self-interested ways of being and doing.

Have you ever noticed what percentage of your thoughts is based on self-doubt or concern about not getting what you want? Or that the people with the lowest self-esteem tend to be those easiest offended? Why, because they have the most self-doubt. Think for a moment of how the need . . .

to achieve can come from a feeling of inadequacy

to micromanage from feeling out of control

to seek pleasure from a feeling of not having enough

to play the victim from a feeling of powerlessness, or

to be overly friendly from a feeling of not being accepted.

Of course not all your mental models are based on insecurity, but many of the more important ones driving your life are. They are your meta-mental models, also known as cocoons, rackets, issues, or trips. It is the place where you hang out, the way of "doing life" that you repeat over and over again. Again, some of these serve you well, while others get in your way. Here, however, I want to focus on the ones that cause you problems, the ones that *are* based in the insecurity of the lesser spirit. Some typical ones include

I am better than	I know better
I am worse than	I can't trust anyone but myself
I must be seen as	I can never do anything right
I deserve	I can't make a difference
I don't have the experience	I am afraid of being average
I have no boundaries	I don't take emotional risks
I must be in control	I must do for everyone else

They are also called boxes. They are socialized self-images that you adopt, and that you hold by constantly promoting or defending them. They are your routine ways of dealing with not being enough, and they are difficult to see. You can become so fused to these ideas that they become your identity, and then you work hard to keep up that appearance and to get what you want.

Exercise 3: How much do you doubt?

From the mental chatter that you noted in Exercise 2, what percentage of the overall chatter is doubt-based, meaning negative, comparative, or coming from an underlying fear?

Our deeper, more problematic mental models often come from childhood events or experiences in the first phase of life that still run our lives.

When I was just six years old my father passed away. He had suffered from an illness as a child and never fully recovered. As an adult he was too weak to hold a full-time job so we lived with his mother, my grandmother. She ran a foster home. Over the years more than a hundred children passed through her country farmhouse, and they all adored her. She was powerful, larger than life, and tough but also compassionate. I was her absolute favorite, even among the grandchildren, and she gave me great comfort after my father died. But soon she too passed away quietly in her sleep one Mother's Day (go figure).

This was a lot of loss for me, and as a result, I took on an abandonment issue that for years manifested as being cautious, aloof, and reserved. I dared not risk the pain of losing someone dear again, so I would protect myself by withdrawing, not fully engaging—and then justifying it through some version of "being independent" or "being cool." It was the only way I knew how to be accepted without ever taking a chance.

Another example is of a woman I know who was ignored as a child and felt "not seen" or not as recognized as she believed she should be. She adopted an "I must be seen attitude." She constantly fought for attention and identity, and was always sensitive to how the world saw her.

We all somehow acquire such a wound in childhood. As a result, we adopt identities, or boxes, early on that serve the needs of being accepted in the adult world rather than attending to the deeper needs of our inner

We all somehow acquire such a wound...no matter how subtle—and an unexamined adult life is often just a reflection of it.

selves. This continues when as adults we constantly look for affirmation outside ourselves for something we imagine we lack within, and it sets us up for problems later on.

In my abandonment issue, for example, whenever I became vulnerable with someone I experienced an overwhelming fear that I would be left. I married out of that fear, thinking that matrimony would be safe and stable, and my fear of being left would go away. Instead, it simply went underground only to resurface later. Similarly, the woman who was ignored and passed over as a child lived as an adult in constant vigilance for signs of respect and ached the days when there was a violation. She too married out of her wound, believing that in some way respect and identity could be found in the relationship.

Did I forget to say that we married each other? We did, and for years we hid our issues in the security we imagined we had found in each other.

Even the most privileged of childhoods brings a wound of some sort—no matter how subtle—and an unexamined adult life is often just a reflection of it. This wound manifests as an acquired habitual defense of the injured child within that we unconsciously continue to act out—even into late age.

It's also nature's way, if you choose to look, to make sure that you continue to grow. *If you suffer no pain, you will never long for freedom.*

Exercise 4: What is your wound? (the Lifeline activity)

The first step in knowing yourself is to reflect on your personal history. As we discussed, your attitudes, talents, and perspectives on life have developed over time from early on. Parents, family, and friends have played important parts in shaping your views. Personal achievements and certain events have also played important roles. In this exercise, try to look deeply into the relationships, events, and achievements that have shaped your life.

1. On a piece of paper, develop a three-part timeline of your life. Plot the timeline on a two-dimensional chart, with the horizontal axis

showing time and the vertical one showing positive and negative impact. The timeline extends from the earliest points in childhood to the present. See the example of my lifeline below.

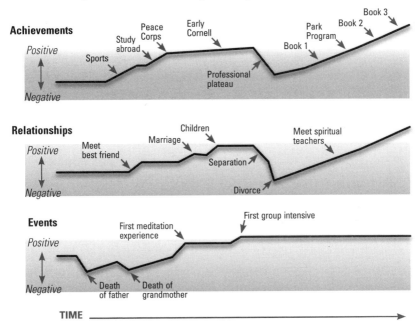

2. Put events that directly influenced your social and personal development along the top line. The focus of this line is on relationship issues that might include moving to a different house, loss of friends, or divorce of parents.

3. The second line shows achievements through your life. These are events or situations surrounding major successes and failures, such as graduating from college, or the first job being a disaster.

4. The third line describes events that don't fall neatly into the relationship or achievement category but somehow had a profound impact on you. An inheritance, the death of a friend, a sudden insight, or a spiritual experience might fall into this category.

The second part of this exercise brings your wounds to the surface, to help you deepen your understanding and self-insight.

1. What was the impact of each of these important relationships, achievements, and events in shaping your mental models, your ideas of yourself, and how you are in the world? Write your reflections about this and the questions that follow on another piece of paper or, better yet, in a journal you'll use for these exercises.

2. What are the patterns or evolutionary lines you see?

3. What wound might you have that is a recurring life issue? How has it influenced your life?

4. What is its source?

But they are not real

Have you ever met someone who made some minor offense on your first meeting and then you shut them out before ever really knowing them? Or known someone who felt mistreated as a child, and now doesn't trust others? Or stereotyped someone based on a first impression? These ideas are based on facts, but the continuing reaction is a fixed interpretation of them—a box. Many of your mental models do not necessarily represent your current reality, although you believe them to *be* your reality. In this sense, it's not necessarily what really happens that makes you suffer, it's your continuing story about these events afterwards that makes you suffer.

> It's not necessarily what really happens that makes you suffer, it's your continuing story about these events afterwards that makes you suffer.
>
> •

For me, my father didn't abandon me, he simply passed away. My pain comes from years of reacting to that event in ways that affected many of my more intimate relationships. Similarly, my now-former wife who felt ignored as a child wanted to be seen and respected. We both in our own ways continued to interpret our world through an idea based on an old event. And who or what made us do that? It was the old wounds that were still running our lives.

If instead of doing this you open yourself up to new life experiences, your boxes can change. For instance, I used to have a simple one around cottage cheese. When I was a boy my mother forced me to eat it and I disliked it so much that I would gag. But at one of my early meditation retreats, I moved from detesting cottage cheese to loving cottage cheese, simply by opening up, clearing my mind, and letting go of that old idea. Maybe being hungry and not having another choice had something to do with it, but anyway, it worked.

A more complex box I lived in for quite a while had to do with my ideas of leadership. My early notions were that leadership is all about how to be skillfully in charge. Then one day a colleague pointed out to me, "How is a maintenance worker whose pride in his work is contagious to others any less of a leader than a CEO? It's more about an attitude and less about skills." My mental model flipped on the spot.

The very first time that I was conscious of breaking mental models was when I studied abroad—the trip I wrote about in the introduction was from that time. I had grown up and was educated in a small town in upstate New York, was in my early twenties, and until then had only traveled out of the Northeast once on a spring break road trip to Florida. My world was quite small.

But then as a graduate student I enrolled in a French-speaking exchange program in Belgium and lived there and traveled throughout Western Europe for well over a year. I didn't know French so I had to learn it as I went along. I hitchhiked extensively, became fluent in the language, and made lot of diverse and interesting friends from many different cultures—Belgian, French, Scandinavian, Turkish, Mexican, Dutch, and so on.

This was my first experience in real personal change, and it was a lesson I would hold dear for years to come. In immersing myself into a new language and new cultures, I had a sense in trying new things that I was starting all over again. There were no established roles or expectations to live by, and I felt a tremendous freedom to experiment with everything. I found the experience of food more aesthetic (it was cuisine and there was no fast food), politics more liberal (we even talked about Marx), sexuality more open (fewer games), and life attitudes more balanced (everyone was home for dinner, and sometimes lunch too). I learned to cook, I learned to dance, I learned to be a little outrageous . . . but most importantly, I learned a great deal about my deeper interests, other ways of living, and the influence of culture and language on my perspectives. I found French, for instance, a far more emotionally expressive language than English, and found myself less reserved too. As a result, my world expanded, and my whole self-concept and demeanor began to shift.

So my reality changed as my mental models changed.

> Consider then, that
> if any one of your
> mental models is
> not true, maybe
> none of them are.
> •

Look for yourself. Where have your ideas, attitudes, or mental models of things changed over the years? Consider then, that if any one of your mental models is not true, maybe none of them are. What does that say about your reality? The life you are living is "a" reality, but it is not THE reality.

Exercise 5: Loosening your mental models

It's actually quite amazing how, when you become aware of a mental model, it loses some or most of its power over you.

1. Take some time to slow down during the day and note, as they come into your awareness, any of the mental models that you wrote down earlier.

2. Bring your attention to them, and notice what happens to their influence. Do they become stronger, weaker, or remain the same?

3. Pick a negative one, and create an alternative reality for it by reframing it in a positive way. Make the reframing plausible, because if it's not plausible, you won't believe it. For instance, if you have one about feeling trapped or not being free, envision a world where your sense of freedom comes from inside of you instead of outside.

4. As you focus your attention on the new way you frame the situation, what impact does that have on the strength of your habitual mental model?

And they cause problems

The sad story is that you live your life through these self-centered mental models and often don't know it. Have you, for instance, ever had a job that feels lame, or a relationship that consistently annoys you, or a pet peeve that sometimes gets the better of you? These feelings are often caused by your mental models not matching up to reality or your inner truth, and they stop you from exploring other ways of being even though you appear to be free. As said before, some of these mental models are useful—you can't function in life without them—but others cause you problems.

They are self-limiting

You are in a box, but you don't know you are in a box. A friend once told me that life is like being stuck inside a cereal box with your goal being to get out of that box, but the directions on how to get out are written on the outside. Being unaware that you are even in a box, you respond to your world based on your scripted notions of what you can or cannot do or what you should or should not do. You want to walk down the same old calf path without questioning it.

> For men are prone to go it blind
> Along the calf paths of the mind;
> And work away from sun to sun
> To do what other men have done.   —Samuel Foss

As we discussed before, the most common self-limiting belief is "I'm not good enough." Other common ones include, "I'm not creative," "That's not *my* job," and "We don't do that here." If you really believe any of them, you'll make that into your reality. A more subtle example might be a financial manager who sees a problem from the perspective of his specialized point of view, while a product manager looks at the same problem from hers. They may get stuck in their respective views, and make themselves reactive and powerless to do anything else. When you have a hammer, everything looks like a nail. You may also know this as tunnel vision.

In leadership development work, I see people limit themselves all the time. One of the biggest challenges I run into is to get people to attend a workshop. Many resist with boxes of "Leadership can't be learned" or "That's too touchy-feely for me" or some other story they like. Yet, *without fail,* when such folks *do* attend, the light bulbs come on—their paradigms shift, and they become huge fans.

One young faculty member came up to me at noon on the first day of a five-day program to say that if she hadn't car-pooled that day she would be leaving already. By the end of that day, however, she said she would return for the following day; by mid-week she was thrilled at what she was learning; and on the last day she asked how she could include leadership development for her research team in her grant proposal to the National Science Foundation.

Self-limitation is perhaps most apparent in career choices. I work with some students, for instance, who won't try for a particular professional opportunity that they really want because they feel they have a certain deficiency, or aren't prepared, or fear being rejected. I also see plenty of others in similar situations who actually land the job and succeed by sheer force of their own passion for it. The ones who won't even try give in to their box, follow the groove, and take themselves out of the game before even trying. In essence, they become bystanders, and forgo a richer life experience.

I often hear claims like "I want to be an engineer," "I want to be a teacher," "I want to be a banker." My question is, How do you know?

Do you want a job, a career or a calling?
•

Did you frame your choices around working to live, or living to work? Do you want a job *(I need to put bread on the table),* a career *(I want to make money and be respected for what I do)* or a calling *(my vocation is my avocation)*? Furthermore, do you ever think about crafting your work to who you are? These are important questions. Too often we make choices based on what we think we should do as opposed to what we are inspired to do, at the cost of our happiness and long-term success.

My early career choices were totally mindless. In the late fall of my senior year in high school my mother asked me if I intended to go to college. When I said yes, she replied, "Well you better apply!" So I applied to two schools at the last minute because of my interest in their wrestling programs.

They asked for my intended major, but I didn't understand even half of the options. So I decided on business because I thought it would eventually get me a job. I graduated but then went on to get my MBA because I wasn't ready to move on and had a girlfriend in town. Afterwards, I avoided professional life until I married someone else, because I wanted to experience the world more.

Then, inspired by my new role as a husband, I used my degrees to land a position in the credit division of a Fortune 100 company, worked hard, and quickly gained recognition. Thinking that the most successful career route in the company was in sales, I leveraged my early success to switch and soon became the number four salesman in the country. I was moving fast. Yet in spite of my achievements, I was bored, totally unfulfilled, and not looking forward to Monday mornings. I just wanted to bail . . . and eventually I did.

In short, I was mechanically driven by my roles, my need to meet the expectations of others, and my early ideas of success. This exercise might help you figure out some of those things a lot quicker than I did.

Exercise 6: Assessing your work

1. How do you feel about the work that you do?
2. Are you spending more of your time with "have tos" or "want tos"?
3. Do you do it because you like it or because you feel you should?
4. Are you doing it for the experience or because it's what you really want? If you are just getting the experience, how long will you put what you really want on hold? Is it worth it?
5. Are you doing it to be good at something you don't like, or to be great at something you really love?
6. Would you say it's a job, a career, or a calling?

They cause stress

Is there anything you relate to that doesn't produce a reaction of attachment (what you want), aversion (what you don't want), or indifference (you don't care)? I bet you can't name one. And when the world doesn't line up with what you want, do you ever become anxious, irritable, or judgmental? Who's to blame, for instance, for the traffic jam you were in this morning? Was it the traffic, or was it you because you didn't leave early enough? Our self-concern results in our objectifying our ideas as concrete or real and people as things or tools, and when they depart from our script, we get upset.

> When the world does not conform to our view, we tend to erupt in judgment, blame, and irritation…
>
> •

When the world does not conform to our view, we tend to erupt in judgment, blame, and irritation, and not take personal responsibility for our feelings. I have this issue about waiting in lines, for instance—that causes me endless suffering. I don't care if it's the cashier, the traffic, or the airport, any time I have to wait for someone else I become very impatient and irritable. It's the flip side to my desire for freedom—I feel contained and out of control, so I start to blame everyone else for what they're doing wrong.

These reactions are my defense mechanisms. Defense mechanisms are automatic responses that we use to defend what we believe ourselves and our world to be. They reduce our anxiety and stress by shifting the burden of responsibility and protecting us from being consciously aware of a thought or feeling that we can't tolerate. Let's say you're angry with someone because they are very critical of you. Here are some typical defenses you might use, along with my personal examples:

Denial: You completely reject the thought or feeling—"They don't know me!"

Suppression: You are vaguely aware of the thought or feeling, but try to hide it—"I'm going to try to be nice."

Blaming or *judgment:* You shift the burden—"He doesn't have a clue."

Rationalization: You come up with various explanations to justify the situation—"He's so critical because he's sucking up to the boss."

Sublimation: You redirect the feeling into unproductive activity— "I'm going drinking."

The problem is that in trying to deal with the stress, these defenses distort the truth. They do that by hiding a variety of your thoughts, feelings, attitudes, or boxes that are their cause to begin with. Your reactivity prevents you from opening up and seeing the true reality.

Worse, you project this reactivity into the world, act on it as truth, and then your "actual" experience "validates" what you believed in the first place. Your mind "spins" the situation in keeping with your fears, and your fears become self-fulfilling. In other words, you create your own reality.

If I have doubts about something, for instance, I will not act with confidence; others will pick up on my lack of confidence and hesitate in turn. *Negativity is reflected by more negativity, defensiveness by more defensiveness, and attempts to control by more resistance.* On the other hand, if I project openness and genuine optimism, the world seems to become more willing to explore the possibilities of what I'm putting forward. Have you ever noticed, for instance, that if you just smile, others become more open, even accommodating?

Exercise 7: What are your defenses?

1. What are some of the typical defenses to your stress and anger? Call them triggers.
2. What are the causes?
3. How do people and events respond to them?

They make problems in relationships

A colleague and I had a bit of disagreement. We never talked about the central point of it because I felt that our conversations were always longer than necessary, and even though the issue seemed important to him, I just didn't want to be bothered. He sensed my veiled indifference and reacted as if I didn't care, despite my half-hearted attempts to placate him. I then reacted by feeling justified in seeing him as needy and high-maintenance (just as I thought to begin with, of course). So I blamed, rationalized, and became dismissive, and even began to pull others into agreeing with my view; meanwhile, he did the same.

The cycle just repeated as we unconsciously colluded in going back and forth, reinforcing our respective points of view, and blowing things out of proportion without ever revealing our real stories and learning the deeper truth. Our relationship suffered and our understanding of the truth suffered. It's a classic example of how what we put out into the world comes back to us—how our reactivity and negativity become self-fulfilling prophecy.

My actions in treating him this way were based on an idea of what I wanted from him. There were parts of the relationship I found valuable and didn't want to give up, but his need to hammer everything out in excruciating detail required way too much of my time. I put this person in a box—made him an object—and the result was a cost to me *(I don't feel good about myself in the way I'm handling it)*, to the relationship *(it's not going well)*, and to the truth *(it's difficult to understand what's really going on)*. As a result, we both stopped learning and growing in the relationship. We didn't like suffering but we did seem to like the innocence we granted ourselves in it by feeling right and justified. Instead of trying to understand, we were just trying to avoid blame by appearing pure. So I prized my suffering and sustained it by refusing to give in or to open.

In this way of relating, we make ourselves alone and unhappy—even more so than when we began.

Exercise 8: Looking at a difficult relationship

1. Is there someone in your life who is particularly problematic for you?
2. If so, what are the triggers?
3. How might you be objectifying them—what box are you putting this person in?

4. If so, what happens when this person challenges, threatens, or reinforces this box?

5. What's it like to live with you when you're using this box?

6. What are the costs of relating to this person this way?

So, just as we do with the world in general, we see that we also objectify people through our mental models. When we objectify someone we treat them as an object instead of a person. *We see them as either having what we want (attachment), being in the way of what we want (aversion), or irrelevant to what we want (indifference).* When you treat people like this, they see it and respond in kind. Even when your behavior is correct but your intent is not, others pick up on it and feel the lack of sincerity—in, for instance, a compliment or an apology that feels insincere, or an attempt to listen that feels as if you don't care, or a personal interest question that seems superficial. It's inauthentic, others sense it, and close down and resist. *People respond to your being, not your behavior,* because they can see through the behavior.

When you live through your boxes this way, you fool yourself because you hang on to your particular view, don't see yourself as part of the equation, and fail to appreciate the other person's perspective. When you have a problem with someone, for instance, your self-centered boxes skew and distort everything because your automatic reaction is to make yourself right and make them wrong without ever really listening to them. As a result, you cut yourself off from their side of the story, and in so doing, from the full truth.

I have even been guilty of objectifying my children, especially my daughter when she was a teenager. Yes, this is true.

She like many teenagers had problems picking up after herself. I was a single parent, and within twenty minutes of returning from her mother's I could tell every place she had been in the house. It was like a dog marking her territory. I grew increasingly frustrated with it and interpreted her mess as a lack of self-discipline. Self-discipline was something I had always used to compensate for my abandonment issue (I would depend on no one).

So my attitude was that she was going to learn the same and be the way I wanted her to be—I put her in a box and treated her like an object. She started treating me likewise; a huge tug-of-war ensued, and it spilled over into other aspects of our relationship. She suffered, I suffered, and our relationship deteriorated. More on this later.

They separate us from ourselves

A very famous philosopher visited an old master. "Master," he said, "I have no peace of mind." The master replied, "Let me hear what you know already, and after hearing you, I will answer you as best as I can."

The philosopher then listed the areas of knowledge in which he was proficient. "Master, I know every science and every art in the world—metaphysics, physics, astronomy, chemistry, biology, psychology, aesthetics, ethics, culture, religion, and philosophy. There is nothing I do not know, but I have no peace of mind."

The great master replied, "All this that you have learned is a bundle of words, with no content inside. You have smeared yourself with a veneer, but you are quite different from that which you have gathered on to yourself. The shirt is not the person and, therefore, your learning and your accomplishments are not what you truly are."

Underlying all our problems is the fact that these boxes of self-concern separate us not only from our world and other people, but also from ourselves. Yours are your conditioned responses that set you apart from the real, authentic you and cause confusion and anxiety.

> Our boxes can make us acquisitive, ambitious, and pleasure-seeking, but not necessarily happy.
> •

We are often confused about happiness, for instance, because we really don't know what we want in the first place. Our boxes can make us acquisitive, ambitious, and pleasure-seeking, but not necessarily happy. You may find some happiness in these things, but is it enduring? Fulfilling personal desires and ambitions in pursuit of things in your outer world doesn't compare to loving relationships, satisfying work, or helping someone in need. The pleasures of your outer world are short-lived, confining your hungry spirit to an endless and increasingly empty loop of frivolous activity.

Exercise 9: What makes you happiest?

1. Look back through your life—events, relationships, accomplishments, activities, acquisitions—and list everything that has made you happy, made you really glow.
2. When were you happiest?
3. Was it when you focused on others making you happy, or when you were making others happy?
4. Was it when you were giving to others or something greater, or was it when you got something or were the center of applause?
5. Was it personal-pleasure-based or other-based?
6. How long did it last?

Your hungry spirit will not give you peace until you begin to understand this one simple thing: You get stuck because your grip of self-concern develops an acquired self-image that you want to project and defend, but this is not who you really are; *this is just an idea of who you are.*

No wonder we make dumb choices. Our happiness doesn't come from acquiring anything at all, only from understanding our own selves.

Thinking that happiness can come from something we acquire can lead to some pretty dumb choices. Trust me. But if it doesn't come from there, where might it come from? The longer I live, the more I believe it comes from understanding how to live my life in keeping with who I really am.

Here again, I use myself as an example.

As mentioned earlier, I arrived in my thirties believing I had a great life. Everything was working perfectly, in keeping with what I had learned to do and expect up to that point. Yet, just underneath the surface was the fact that I had married out of fear, achieved to meet the expectations of others, and parented in a way that laid my own unmet needs on my children. Much of who I thought I was, to that point, was rooted in my abandonment box—which had gone underground for years and only manifested in my life as a rebellious desire for freedom and independence. But it came rushing to the surface when my wife started to pull away with her own issue. (I can still hear the alarm bells going off!) Suddenly the veneer of who I thought I was got stripped away, leaving me painfully revealed and with many, many unanswered questions.

Instead of feeling my "normal" fortunate and confident, I felt insecure and lost. I began to doubt, and my world began to doubt me in return. I started to make poor choices—tried to sell the house, started dating too soon, pushed away the children at a time when they too were suffering—and those choices led to even greater doubt. Everything spiraled down.

I soon felt abandoned in *every* aspect of my life—my wife left me, my work wasn't going well, my friends, family, and even children distanced themselves. My wound had become a self-fulfilling prophecy. I felt abandoned, so the world did its counterpoint in return. Yes, this was my mid-life crisis; and it was brought on by the collapse of who I thought I was. My life issue was raging out of control as I had no place to hide from it anymore. It was like the Universe took me by the shoulders and shook me saying, "Deal with this!"

As Dante said, "In the middle of the journey of our life I came to myself within a dark wood where the straight-way was lost."

Exercise 10: Who am I?

1. Ask yourself, "Who am I?" You can't do that with a lot of people around. So go to your room, shut your door, turn off your cell phone, and ask the question.

2. Ask it at least ten to twenty times and write down your answers. Don't overthink it—just let the first thought be your best thought each time you ask.

3. As you proceed, see if you notice something about yourself that's contrary to what you have thought, or reveals a deeper longing.

2

The Freedom of the Greater Spirit: You Can Choose another Way

"I am not what happened to me, I am what I choose to become."

—Carl Jung

You can change your mental models

One of the leading meditation teachers in the west, Jack Kornfield, tells the story a man who planned a peaceful, solitary meditation retreat in a cabin in the woods. As he began his practice, he heard the gurgling of a brook nearby. As time went on, this gurgling seemed to grow louder and louder, and it began to disturb his peace of mind. He found his thoughts constantly following the sound of the brook and he started to crave the silence he believed he was missing. He grew frustrated. At one point the sound became so unbearable for him, that he went into the water and started moving the rocks around!

Instead of looking within to find peace of mind, he tried manipulating his world to make it conform to his box. This is like cleaning the mirror when what you really need to do is wash your face. It's not by moving rocks that you find happiness—it's by transforming your relationship to them.

> Instead of looking within to find peace of mind, he tried manipulating his world to make it conform to his box.
>
> •

The good news is that once you become aware of your boxes you can begin to change them. Certain things that happen in your life are out of your control, but you do have a choice on how you respond to them—and therein is your opportunity. As holocaust victim and psychologist Viktor Frankl once said, "Between stimulus and response there is a space. In that space is our power to choose our response. In that response lays our growth and our freedom."

The problem, then, is not in having expectations of the world—it's what you do when your expectations are not met. Your experience of life is determined by a combination of *events plus your response* to those events.

Experience = Events + Response

Rather than reacting and digging in when events don't comply with what you want, you could notice your reaction, choose a different response, and make the situation more workable. For example, instead of complaining about the problems you have because you don't have enough information, or with this person who isn't doing the job right, you can choose to stop blaming and stressing, and work to see other possibilities. Your awareness is the key. This does not mean giving up; it means there are multiple ways to go, and you can move on without the drama.

When trouble arises, ask yourself: Are you seeking understanding or just strengthening your aversion by blaming others or the situation? For instance, instead of a having a knee-jerk reaction to a person you continue to have problem with, ask whether you are there to learn something or just to make the other person wrong. Something as simple as that is often enough to diffuse a situation. Then, depending on how skillful you are, it might invite the other person to do the same. You might both learn to grow in the relationship and make it more workable.

In another classic Zen story, the master has a stick and says to the student, "If you say this is a stick, I will hit you. If you say this is not a stick, I will hit you. If you say nothing about the stick, I will hit you." The student comes many days in a row and says the wrong thing and is hit with the stick every time. He becomes so frustrated and angry, that one day he finally takes the stick away from the master. The master bows and says, "The next lesson begins tomorrow."

If you consciously choose to respond in a different way, you can gain your freedom. You continue to suffer from the events in your life not because they continue to disturb you, but because of your own view of them.

Exercise 11: Working with your defenses

1. Think back to some of your triggers in Exercise 7 (page 41). What provoked your response?
2. How did this make you feel?
3. What insecurities were underlying your response?
4. Was there another response you could have chosen? Could you have empathized, inquired, disengaged, or disclosed something?
5. Is the unfairness you experienced your excuse for how you reacted, or do you feel empowered to do something about it?

Where you suffer often gives the clue

Have you ever had your hot button pushed in the same type of situation again and again? Been drawn to the same type of lover over and over but your needs are not met? Felt stuck in the same area of your life without change? Gotten into the same conflict again and again in your relationship with someone?

These repeated patterns are often your boxes coming under attack and could be signs for you to wake up and make a choice. Carl Jung said, "Whatever shadows we don't want to see in ourselves, life will bring to us as destiny." It's like Bill Murray in the film *Groundhog Day*, waking up in the same day over and over until he learned what he needed to do in that day. The same events kept repeating themselves until he finally "got" what he was supposed to do in each situation. Sound familiar?

> These repeated patterns are often your boxes coming under attack and could be signs for you to wake up and make a choice.
>
> •

For example, I used to be invisible in groups because I was afraid of looking or saying something stupid. At times I would have something to say but would wait, being unsure, until someone else would finally say it.

Then I would regret it, but my life kept putting me into these situations.

This went on for years and I started to feel that this way of being was holding me back. I wanted to stretch myself but knew I would have to force the issue because, in spite of my intentions, I would continue to be a bystander. So I started to take on the facilitator role wherever I could and, over time, my anxiety in groups gradually dissolved. Group participation and facilitation are now central to my work.

I have a friend who was stuck in a pattern that got him fired four times over the course of five years. He insisted on blaming others and the situation, complaining, "Why are there so many screwed-up people and places to work in the world?" Clearly he needed to learn that his problems were not created "out there" and that he needed to examine his boxes "in here."

When you see a repeated pattern like this in your life, it's like you're calling forth a certain reality because your hungry spirit wants to complete itself. Your boxes are causing you to suffer and you're being reminded to wake up. Your suffering is a necessary signal to choose your freedom (from how you limit yourself) and grow. Carl Jung said our negative patterns "must be understood, ultimately, as the suffering of a soul which has not discovered its meaning." And, as Joseph Campbell added, "Where you stumble, there your treasure lies."

So pay attention to these feelings and use them as signs to wake up and do your life a different way. My friend who kept losing his job, for instance, learned that he was self-sabotaging through his version of the "I can't make a difference" box. With the support of some of his friends, he learned to check himself and is now very successful.

Exercise 12: Find your repeated patterns
  1. Where might there be repeated patterns like this in your life?
  2. How might you be stuck and not open in the areas where they take over?
  3. Where do you consistently have problems in relationships?

4. What fear might you be covering up, or what needs might you be holding onto instead of letting life fulfill them?

5. Can you choose a different response? What can you do differently?

Yet choosing is still difficult

It's not easy to let go of something, even if you are fully aware of it. Have you tried? Awareness helps make your boxes less solid, but awareness alone is often not enough to free you. That's because your issues are linked to your feelings of self-concern. You are more able to make these choices when you feel good about yourself, and have some confidence and emotional strength. Your efforts to change won't take hold if they're still rooted in trying to get what you want from the world. You'll just revert back to old ways of being.

Getting out of the box isn't only about making choices on how you respond to your world, but also on how you feel about yourself and what makes you happy. You need to replace your old boxes with newer, healthier ones that tap into your feelings of self-worth rather than self-concern. The good news is that your hungry spirit is incredibly fertile ground for planting your new intentions in: What you feed into it and focus it on is what grows out of it. Working with its energy in the right way, you can create a new reality.

Because you first must find your basic goodness

This is where many of the New Age and self-help change-your-world books and programs start to be misleading. It's important, essential really, to understand that *there is both a lesser and greater hungry spirit.*

Negative emotions like anger, fear, desire, jealousy, pride, and so on make up the lesser spirit. For the most part, these emotions are all based on getting or not getting what you want from the world. The selfish cravings that you adopt in the pursuit of things you want are precisely what cause you endless suffering when you don't get them. As Buddhists like to say, "Selfishness is the root to all sorrow." This *self-concern* is designed to protect and preserve your ideas of yourself and it's rooted in your *survival instinct*. It is a necessary function—you don't want to get rid of it. But at times it holds you back when you need to be moving on.

Positive emotions such as love, joy, interest, gratitude, and enthusiasm make up the greater spirit and are much more inclusive and outward-oriented. They open you, broaden your view, connect you to others, and extend you into the world. They are what make you feel best about yourself. This *greater-concern* is designed to help you grow and adapt, and is rooted in your *evolutionary instinct*.

Tibetan spiritual master Trungpa Rinpoche called these positive emotions your basic goodness. It is the highest expression of your hungry spirit and your most authentic self. The inspiration from and belief in your own basic goodness is what gives you confidence to make choices that serve the best you possible.

> To create a new reality, you simply must discover this basic goodness. You can't break up, erase, or just let go of old boxes and mental models—you have to transform them by . . . coming from that stronger place.
> •

To create a new reality, you simply must discover this basic goodness. You can't break up, erase, or just let go of old boxes and mental models—you have to transform them by transmuting the energy of the hungry spirit into coming from that stronger place.

How do you do this? It's a simple, elegant trick: Engage the world in ways that lessen the grip of your self-concern. As you shift your focus from yourself to others and to causes in your outer world, it's amazing: Good feelings arise inside, and your basic goodness begins to shine through.

Albert Schweitzer said, "We don't change, we just stand more revealed." These growing feelings of goodness give you a sense of worthiness and transform the diversions of the lesser spirit. In essence, you find yourself by losing yourself in something greater (your self-concern in your greater-concern). This may seem counter-intuitive, but it's true.

Again, your negative emotions often show you where to begin. For instance, when you get frustrated from not getting what you want from the world you could shift the focus from yourself to the point of view of the other. Instead of being impatient with the cashier, I *could* ask how his or her day is going. In putting myself in the cashier's shoes, I sidestep my self-concern and allow myself to give instead of get. Good feelings arise, my petty frustrations fade away, and the cashier may even respond in a positive way. In the same way, when I used to come home from a bad day at work, I would at times sit down, have a drink, and fester; but when instead I turned my attention to the children and their day, my worries disappeared.

I once belonged to a men's group and would often go to our meetings feeling miserable and weighed down by problems at work, the challenges of single parenting, and other uncertainties I was facing at the time. In entering that space with other men, whenever we focused on my stuff, I left feeling no better, maybe even a little worse. But when we focused on someone else's issues, and I placed my attention on them, I felt uplifted. In trying to understand and offer comfort for their challenges, my own problems seemed to lose their grip, and I would always walk away feeling a lot better.

Try it yourself. When you become frustrated with someone, choose to be kind instead of angry and watch what happens to you inside. This may not work in all cases for you, but it will in many. Another way to look at this is to ask whether happiness makes you kind, or if being kind makes you happy? Interesting question isn't it? Studies show that acts of kindness and altruism lead to greater happiness. Why? Because they take the focus of your concern off yourself and place it on someone else. Try truly empathizing with another person, or giving them something without expectation in return, and see what happens. Again, good feelings are likely to arise, including positive self-regard and happiness. Try to recognize them as they do: This is your basic goodness. Compare that to getting a new a new car, or a new outfit. Which feeling is greater or more enduring?

The basic strategy, then, for discovering your basic goodness, and a deeper happiness, is to move from a self-centered world to a more other-centered world. In simple terms

> What opens you makes you happy
>
> What closes you makes you suffer

Exercise 13: What opens and closes you?

1. Review your answers to Exercise 9 (page 45), and ask which activities and interactions opened you and which closed you.
2. Under each one, list the different activities or interactions it involves.
3. Review the lists, asking which of the activities or interactions in it open you and which ones close you.
4. What adjustments might you make in any or all of these areas to become happier?

In commenting on how he achieved greater happiness, philosopher Bertrand Russell said: "Gradually I learned to be indifferent to myself and my deficiencies; I came to center my attention increasingly upon external objects: the state of the world, various branches of knowledge, individuals for whom I felt affection." If you pursue happiness it will elude you, but if you focus on your family, your friends, your work, and doing your very best with them, happiness will find you.

> All the joy the world contains
>
> Has come through wishing well for others
>
> All the misery the world contains
>
> Has come through wanting pleasure for oneself
>
> —Shantideva

Exercise 14: Moving to an other-centered world

1. Select in advance a few meetings or conversations that you know you are going to have. Commit to try focusing, when the time

comes, on what that person is feeling and saying, and how you might help them. When you do meet or speak with them, deliberately try to make their day brighter.

2. While you are at work, select a task or activity that involves others and try helping them with it instead of focusing only on your own effort.

3. Though it probably sounds like a cliché, try practicing random acts of kindness—a sweet gesture, a smile, a simple gift, or doing something for someone.

4. How do these make you feel inside?

What is this basic goodness, really?

Ask yourself, what's the most meaningful thing you've done in the last week, month, year, or in life so far? Where have you felt most deeply? Why is that the most important thing? Ask why over and over again until you come to the something that begins to tug on your heart. When you find it, my bet is that it is something related to feeling alive and compassionate. That feeling is a taste of your basic goodness.

All the world's major belief systems talk about this. Buddhism calls it Buddha nature, in Hinduism it is Shiva, in Greek philosophy it is your Daemon (not demon), and in Christianity it's the "kingdom of God." Each of these is describing a basic quality of human nature that is both awake and compassionate.

Even today's scientists agree that what most distinguishes human beings from other species on the planet is our capacity for both consciousness and empathy, in other words, our ability to be both awake and compassionate. Other mammals exhibit some degree of these, but none come near to what we possess. Awareness and compassion set us apart and represent *the very cutting edge of our evolutionary urge and our longing hungry spirit.* Why? Because they suspend your ideas about yourself,

> What most distinguishes human beings from other species ... is our capacity for both consciousness and empathy ... [they] set us apart and represent the very cutting edge of our evolutionary urge.
>
> •

open you to other, and serve as a foundation for the developing of all your greater faculties.

Basic goodness is the treasure of our existence but we are most often not even aware of it. It is like having a gem in your pocket and mistaking it for an ordinary stone. The gem is not powerless, but failing to recognize it makes it so.

> Being unaware of your basic goodness is like mistaking a gem in your pocket for an ordinary stone.
>
> •

If you stop for just a moment and take a close look, you may see: In spite of all your problems, there is something basically good about you, about your existence as a human being. As we've seen so far, this feeling of goodness doesn't necessarily come from fulfilling basic desires or even from acquiring great things—those feelings are fleeting and ephemeral. This feeling comes from a deeper, more fundamental level. It is a relaxed, gentle, openness that comes from appreciating and connecting to your world in a way that wakes you up and feels good.

As your mind slows down when you relax on a vacation or a walk in the woods, you can see it fairly easily. Gaps in the mental chatter begin to appear, letting your basic nature shine through. You may experience it as a taste of sadness, tenderness, or sympathetic kindness that comes when you make yourself truly responsive to your world and appreciate it just as it is. It lies just below the doubt and fear you carry all day, and all those selfish views that make you cling to, reject, or be indifferent to your experience. If you really calm your mind, you'll see that under the layers of doubt, fear, and busyness is a certain raw goodness that is fundamental and unconditional. Call it God, call it Tao, call it love—we all have it. Just call it.

My first solid taste of basic goodness came while I was in the Peace Corps in Nepal. I traveled to a small village in India to take part in a ten-day meditation retreat. In the first few days of the program, my knees hurt from long periods of sitting and my mind wandered endlessly with pointless chatter. I was growing frustrated and began to doubt whether the retreat was such a good idea.

Gradually, however, my body and mind began to relax. I started to experience gaps between my thoughts, and a light, uplifting feeling began to emerge. I noticed between the periods of sitting how bright the colors of my surroundings were, how great the food tasted, and how wonderful the din of the world was. I felt awake and happy, completely happy. I felt confident but at the same time broken-hearted with compassion for everyone. In fact, I was so blissful that by the tenth day, I was convinced that I just needed two more days to reach enlightenment! Well, in retrospect, I also learned that the delusions of our minds sometimes have no bounds. But the fact remains that as my mind stilled, my basic goodness shined through. The taste of it was so strong that year after year I took meditation retreats to help keep myself in touch with it.

Discovering basic goodness gives birth to trust and confidence in yourself, and that trust and confidence has magic in it. When you come from a place of basic goodness, the world responds in kind. Basic goodness doesn't go away—when you slow down, you can always find it, touch it, feel it. When you have problems, you can draw on it as a source of courage and confidence. When you have issues with others, you know that underneath it all, your tormentors have it too. As you turn to it more and more often, it grows in strength and spreads to other aspects of your life.

> When you come from a place of basic goodness, the world responds in kind.
>
> •

To remove the self-doubt behind your socialized façade, you must ultimately discover what this basic goodness is *for yourself* and *in your own way*. Not only discover it, but nurture it. Most of the rest of this book is about ways you can do that.

Exercise 15: Tasting basic goodness

1. Go back to your answers to the first question in Exercise 9 (page 45), and again ask what is the most meaningful thing you have done in the last week or month—something that made you really glow.

2. Why is that the most important?

3. Keep asking why until you get down to one word or it begins to tug on your heart.

4. How has this operated in your life?

5. How have you used it in difficult times?

6. When you need to let go of something, draw on this basic goodness.

When you find it, you find not only happiness but also success

Moving to a more other-centered world to discover your basic goodness leads not only to greater happiness but also to greater success. In his ground-breaking research, Jim Collins found that the highest performing organizations tend to be led by people who are both driven (not so surprising) and humble (surprising). By humble he meant that they work quietly behind the scenes, serving the mission of the organization and those who are serving that mission. They balance their personal ambition with a dedication to a cause and to others serving it. *And that is a key point: They are both selfish and selfless—driven to succeed while being in service to others.* Highly effective people are not free of self-interest—they just have something else they are working on, too. Something bigger.

Daniel Goleman found something similar in his study of emotional intelligence. He showed that what distinguishes human effectiveness most is the ability to manage emotions in a healthy and productive manner. The foundation for doing that is awareness and empathy—the very essence of the basic goodness described above—and these are qualities that can be learned.

There is now a whole range of studies on human effectiveness that shows overly self-interested ways of being result in problems, while becoming self-aware and opening to other makes for more productive, creative, and adaptive ways.

The simple reason for all this is that one way of operating is rooted in fear and the other in basic goodness. This just makes sense. Think of it: If you're on a team and everyone is playing as a team, the team performs better. The whole is greater than the sum of the individual parts. If everyone plays for themselves, the team performs worse. Are you there for you, or are you there for the others too, and the greater purpose? It's that simple.

In my own many years now of studying leadership, this is easy to see. I have found that those who serve other tend to succeed while those who serve self exclusively tend to derail. It's so predictable. Don't get me wrong, we always act in our own self-interest; but we'll see that it's in our own self-interest to act in the interest of others, too.

> I have found that those who serve other tend to succeed while those who serve self exclusively tend to derail.
>
> •

Great leaders are also serving something other than themselves. Some may get by overly committing to self-interests in the short run, but not over the long haul. As Viktor Frankl said, "Success, like happiness, cannot be pursued, it must ensue . . . as an unintended consequence of one's personal dedication to a course greater than oneself."

Moving closer to a more other-centered world not only enables choice, but also greater happiness and success. In other words, *what makes you happy also makes you successful.*

As I wrote in the introduction, the better you feel about yourself, the more likely you are to extend yourself out and help in positive ways. It's like Mark Twain said, "Whoever is happy, will make others happy too." To live your life from this place is a powerful catalyst for positive change, not only in your life, but in the lives of others too.

PART TWO

Discovering the Basic Goodness
of the Greater Spirit:
New Mental Models for Living

Prefatory for Part Two

*"The desire for happiness is essential to man. It is the motivator of all our acts.
The most venerable, clearly understood, enlightened, and reliable constant in the
world is not only that we want to be happy, but that we want only to be so. Our
very nature requires it."*

—St. Augustine

SO AS I ENTERED MID-LIFE I found myself lost. I felt thrown into an unwanted journey, but at an instinctive level I knew that I had to pay attention in order to make my way out. Eventually, I found my way again. With the added benefit of hindsight, this section draws on some of the lessons I learned about finding happiness and success.

In essence these are new mental models to live by that can help you retrain your mind and heart. Remember: What you focus on in your hungry spirit is what you draw out of it. In practicing these new mental models, you will discover that they connect you to the basic goodness of your greater spirit, while at the same time dissolving the grip of self-concern of your lesser spirit. They not only draw on your basic goodness, they also nurture it. Basically, the path towards and the fulfillment of this basic goodness are one and the same: They strengthen one another simultaneously, like pouring water into water.

3
Wake Up

"To become different from what we are, we must have some awareness of what we are."

— Eric Hoffer

AWARENESS IS NOT ONLY IMPORTANT, it is paramount to achieving any lasting or significant growth. It is also foundational to all the new mental models and exercises that follow. It bears repeating that your boxes are not the source of your problems, but your lack of awareness of them is. When you are self-aware and honest with yourself, you become conscious of your boxes, loosen their grip, and gain insight into other possibilities.

> Awareness is not only important, it is paramount to achieving any lasting or significant growth.
>
> •

Typically, though, we don't see the world as it is. We see it as we want it to be, as filtered through our boxes. This particularly blinds us to seeing who we really are, and helps keep us trapped in the endless loop of habitual patterns. Awareness cuts through this dynamic and allows us to see things freshly, just as they are without being colored by our fear, need, or judgments.

Awareness allows you to see the difference between your habitual patterns and your deeper truths. It helps you identify the boundaries between you and others, so as to better see whose problems are whose and where responsibility for dealing with them lies. It helps you spot the hazards and opportunities of the bigger picture so you can avoid or rise to them.

Awareness also gives you an opportunity to make a choice about how you respond to a particular event. Instead of being defensive when something doesn't go your way, you can consciously play to your strengths while being less concerned about preserving your image or exposing your shortcomings. You no longer need to know everything or always be right because you know where you can contribute. I know, for instance, that I'm not always a person of action but am naturally one of vision—and I don't mind being transparent about that.

Seeing how to manage your strengths and shortcomings like this opens you, relaxes you, and instills a sense of self-confidence that makes everything seem workable. It allows you to be just who you are, and to share what you know and don't know. It's very liberating.

Have you ever noticed that simply admitting to others that you don't know something builds confidence in and of itself? It strips away the false pretense of the self-image, and can be very disarming to others. They see you're not trying to hide anything. It stops the game-playing and allows them to open and trust you.

Awareness also helps you work with the constant barrage of thoughts and feelings chattering away in your heart and mind. I'm speaking again of the chatter that so often leads to a mindless pursuit of things outside ourselves—possessions, experiences, people's opinions of us, and so on. Calming the mind and heart is a first step to cut through this stream of consciousness and create space for the kind of reflection that expands your clarity and awareness. This still, reflective space helps you sort through the chaff for the seed, and to reduce, and ultimately close the gap between appearance (your boxes) and reality. There are many ways to cultivate this space, among them yoga, meditation, church, and solitary exercise. Find what works for you.

In the rest of this chapter I share ways to help increase your awareness. These are the primary ones I've found helpful over the years.

Make reflection a habit

Reflection is essential to developing your awareness because it deepens it. Life changes when you consciously reflect on your experience because *through reflection you can both escape the influence of the past and create the possibilities of the future.* You see more clearly with a settled, reflective mind. I create reflective space every day through meditation and exercise. Others pray, walk, journal, volunteer. Anything that allows you to break up the routine, step back, and take stock is good. Spending time in nature is particularly powerful for many people.

I go on a meditation retreat every year. Lately I've been going every summer for a month. By the end of the school year I'm pretty worn out from all the activity and can barely even think about the possibilities of the next year. Yet, without fail, a week or so into the retreat, I'm feeling totally refreshed and enthused about the coming year and new ideas start popping into my head.

In my field of leadership development and human effectiveness, the power of reflection is often referred to as *retreat, renew, and return*—retreat from the daily spin, renew through reflection on what is really going on, and return with new insight and vigor. This trains the mind to be more aware. It sheds light, and that light creates a sense of optimism that helps us derive meaning, learn, and grow from every experience.

So one of the best things you can do is to *make refection a habit* by creating a regular space for it in your life. Make it a ritual by committing to do something for this purpose every day. It can be as simple as making quiet time for yourself.

At the end of some of the more intense leadership workshops that I lead, I ask people to take twenty minutes of complete silence—no talking, no cell phones, no e-mail, no eye contact, nothing except sitting still or taking a quiet walk. Inevitably the feedback is that was the most powerful part of the day. Why? Because it breaks up the constant spinning and the hurly burly of experience.

Exercise 16: Creating reflective space

> Commit to at least thirty minutes a day that allows you to take time out from your daily routine and take stock. This could be a walk, meditation, exercise, journaling, silent time, prayer, or what have you. Make that time the same time every day and call it your reflective space. Guard it and try not to let other things interfere with that time.

Seek feedback

Leadership guru Tom Peters once said that "feedback is the breakfast of champions." Why? It's essential to our growth. Without feedback, *you know not that you know not*; but with feedback, *you know that you don't know*. Knowing that you don't know is the threshold of change. There is no simpler way to get out of your box than to appreciate another person's point of view. Without feedback, you are often unaware of your hidden strengths, your blind spots, and your impact on others, and therefore unable to make adjustments for them. If I'm perceived in a situation as being aloof, for instance—as I often am because I'm an introvert—I want to know so I can change and be more engaged and approachable.

Feedback is also good because it forces you to deal with your defenses. I don't care who you are, if you receive negative or constructive feedback, your first response is likely to be defensive. Often people deny, rationalize, or blame, and the feedback just bounces off them. Look at your defenses when this happens to you, because they are often clues to how you can wake up. In fact, the stronger your defensive response, the more likely it's pointing to one of your boxes. So suspend your judgment and ask yourself if the feedback really rings true. This takes courage of course, but growth always does.

The perception of others is often as right as it is wrong; but even if wrong, that perception is still a reality to deal with. In the end you are the best judge because others are also working with their own boxes in giving it. Treat what they offer as a gift and ask yourself if there's really something to it.

Exercise 17: Feedback bombardment

I've used this technique often and it is very powerful.

1. Gather a group of friends or colleagues.
2. Select one to go first in receiving feedback from the others.
3. Everyone takes a few moments to think about what they want to say.
4. Then each member of the group says what they appreciate about this person and one thing they wish or hope that person might change. In other words, both positive and constructive feedback.
5. Someone in the group takes notes for the person receiving feedback so that person can just focus on listening.
6. The person is only allowed to ask clarifying questions while receiving the feedback and not to argue or comment. Their attitude should be to take it in as a gift.
7. After receiving feedback from everyone, the person can ask one question to the group as a whole for more information.
8. Switch to the next person and repeat the process.

Meditate for insight

There is a whole canon of research that extols the benefits of meditation. Study after study has shown that meditation has multiple positive effects on your life including reduced stress, better health, enhanced cognitive abilities, more positive emotions, improved relationships, greater creativity and productivity, and heightened awareness and alertness. Personally, I have found it to be an indispensable tool for creating balance, maintaining perspective, and increasing awareness and insight into myself, others, and reality.

While meditating, for instance, you can see a constant stream of thoughts and feelings (boxes) as they arise. The practice is to just to observe them and let them pass by without clinging to, rejecting, or reacting to them in any way. It reveals an underlying joy.

> He who binds himself to joy
> Does the winged life destroy
> But he who kisses the joy as it flies
> Lives in eternity's sun rise
>
> —William Blake

Awareness helps us let go, see how boxes aren't real, and create space in our heart and mind.

•

When I am simply aware like this, thoughts and feelings pop like soap bubbles in the air. Instead of the chatter leaving imprints on the mind, thoughts become traceless like the footprints of birds flying through the sky. Even when something is really bothering me, if I just gently bring my awareness back to whatever it is again and again, insight into what's going on eventually arises; the problem's hold on me begins to loosen. Awareness helps us let go, see how boxes aren't real, and create space in our heart and mind.

This practice also creates a stillness that is open and awake, that helps us be less reactive and more appreciative of our world. I feel a palpable difference in the days I haven't meditated. When I have, things are less sticky—I'm less easily agitated by things that go wrong, and much more appreciative of the things that go right. Even with just twenty minutes in the morning, my mind is sharper, my energy calmer, and my responses to events less reactive because I can make choices. It's like a cleansing: Sounds are clearer, colors are brighter, and food tastes better. I'm much more aware of what I'm feeling and thinking, and more observant of what's going on around me. I pick up on things others don't readily see—who has lost a little weight, or changed their hair color, or was in my office when I was down the hall. Why? There is less noise, less chatter in the mind, and less distraction.

In really deep meditation you may be stripped so clean of distractions that everything appears as a stainless clear texture, almost like a still forest pool. The slightest thought or emotion makes a ripple, breaks it up, and distorts its perfect reflectiveness. The pristine clarity of that space may also bring an experience of profound vulnerability, a raw and tender heart free from layers of illusion, aching with blissful yet still painful joy. This is basic goodness, and it is the stuff that we are made of.

Exercise 18: Meditation

1. Sit in a chair in a comfortable position with your back straight, your feet flat on the floor, and your hands resting in your lap. Keep your head aligned with your spine and your chin pointed slightly down. Instead of using a chair, some people may wish to sit on a cushion; but do so only if you can remain comfortable in that position without moving for twenty to thirty minutes.

2. Bring attention to your breath—on your upper lip as the breath passes in and out of your nostrils, or on your abdomen as it rises and falls with your breathing. Either is fine. Just relax and gently bring your attention to your breath as it moves in and out and notice any sensations that arise at your point of focus: hot, cold, tingling—any sensation at all. Just *be* with your breath and these sensations without reacting. As the mind wanders and begins to think about or feel other things, bring it gently back to the breath and observe.

3. The mind's natural tendency is to wander, so don't become upset at having to return your attention to the breath frequently. Let go of your thoughts and emotions and gently return to the breath. You'll need to let go hundreds and thousands of times, but in bringing your attention back to your breath remember to do so without judgment or aggression. Just gently bring it back and rest your attention on the breath, let go, and relax. Notice the thoughts as they arise, but let them pass through, like the clouds passing in front of the sun.

4. After twenty to thirty minutes, end your session and just notice how you feel.

5. As you go about your day and tension emerges, first notice and then follow your breath. It creates space.

If you are interested in learning more about meditation, I would suggest either attending a meditation center (there are many), or reading *Insight Meditation* by Joseph Goldstein or *Meditation for Beginners* by Jack Kornfield. These books are by trusted teachers and show you how simple it is to start—and stick with—a daily meditation practice. Their instructions are in the *insight* meditation tradition and show you in a step-by-step fashion how to develop the time-honored skill of moment-to-moment mindfulness. Both of them were among my early meditation instructors.

Exercise regularly

Like meditation, exercise also has many physical and emotional benefits. Research shows that it reduces anxiety and stress, lowers the risk of many different diseases, tones and builds the body, increases the quality of life, improves sleep, retards cognitive decline in old age, and produces positive emotions. Why? Your body feels better, you feel like you accomplished something, it breaks up the routine of worry and stress, and it provides a reflective space. I exercise a lot and am refreshed and energized by it, and that makes the rest of my day more productive.

Here, though, I advocate solitary exercise because of its great power in helping to create a reflective space. Have you ever had this experience: Something is bothering you, or you're working on a problem, and you take a break to do some solitary physical activity like walking, jogging, cycling, or whatever . . . and things break loose? In my own case, if I'm on a writing project and go running, I have to take a notepad with me—because I get a rush of insights into what I'm working on. It happens almost every time. There is something about the interaction of the mind and body in physical exercise that breaks up the patterns and lets other things flash through. So, you might want to try it—but don't take your iPod with you. Just leave the mind alone in this space, without distraction, and see what comes up.

Exercise like this is a health builder, a stress reliever, and an insight maker—another very important thing to find space for almost every day. Don't overdo it in the beginning if you're not exercising already, though. Start slowly and build up to about to about 45–60 minutes a day.

Keep a journal

Journaling is another helpful tool. Not everyone is attracted to meditation, and journaling is a great alternative for creating a reflective space. It's one of the oldest methods of self-exploration and discovery, and a powerful exercise for adding awareness, texture, and meaning to your life.

When you write in a journal, you can reach in and be candid about your inner thoughts and feelings. This helps you gain some insight into your boxes. It also helps you tap into your unconscious for a deeper perspective about who you are. It can help you through difficult times to empty your boxes of worry and fears onto paper and try to see where they come from and how you can resolve them. It helps you generate creative ideas, and to develop foresight by remembering and reflecting on past mistakes.

I don't advocate making daily entries of current events like keeping a diary. Rather, I encourage you to use journaling to explore your inner world. I've kept that kind of a journal for many years, and used to write almost daily—particularly during times of stress. It has been tremendously helpful in understanding myself and the processes I go through.

Now I write only when something is bothering me that I can't quite put my finger on. An event or a thought triggers a glimpse or flash of something that I sense is just the tip of something greater that I should write about. So I write my way into it and often the act of writing brings the bigger thing up, and leads to a rush of insight and greater awareness. The combination of the physical and reflective elements of writing somehow stimulates an awareness of things that are just lingering below the surface of consciousness. Something about the process awakens and allows your inner voice to emerge.

Journaling also expands your awareness by allowing you not only to discover your way but also to retrace your journey—to see where you have grown and where you may be stuck. In preparing for this book, for instance, I went back through sixteen years of journals. I half expected to find a continuing drone of traps and issues that I fell into and repeated over and over again. To my surprise, I found real movement, growth, and evolution. I don't believe I would have grown nearly as much without journaling. Now I always keep a journal with me.

Exercise 19: Journaling

I borrowed this technique from Natalie Goldberg. The technique asks you to journal for ten-minute periods while answering a series of questions. The "non-rules" for answering these questions are:

1. *Keep your hand moving.* Don't pause or hesitate to make sure you're making sense. That's your mind trying to take control. If you run out of things to say, then simply write "I don't know what to say" over and over again until something moves you otherwise.

2. *Don't cross out.* That's your internal judge editing and trying to make sense. Even if you didn't mean to write it, leave it. It may provide insight later.

3. *Don't worry about spelling, punctuation, or grammar.* This is the same as above. No one else is going to read this or try to make sense of it, so don't slow yourself down by trying to make it pretty.

4. *Lose control.*

5. *Don't think or get logical.* Remember, you are trying to free your mind.

6. *Go for the jugular.* If something comes up that seems off the wall, go right into it. It probably has deeper meaning. Remember, no one else is going to read it.

Some sample sentence completion questions to try:

1. Five years from now, I am most proud of . . .
2. When my friends talk about me they say . . .
3. Ten years from now I can teach others . . .
4. The 27 things I want to do before I die are . . .

These questions are just a start. If journaling appeals to you, then try to continue on a regular basis. Develop your own questions based on what you wonder about in your life as they come up. After enough practice, you will make the process your own, and it will become a habit and a partner in your growth.

Cultivate mindfulness

If nothing else, simply learn to take interest in your world. Pay attention to and be mindful of the details of your life and how you dress, eat, clean, walk, and do all the other mundane things that you do. Do you ever take time to observe what you're doing, or do you always just do things automatically and without thinking? Could you learn to do them with a little more care or in a way that connects you to your world more directly and simply?

> If nothing else, simply learn to pay attention and be mindful of the details of your life and how you dress, eat, clean, walk . . .
>
> •

For instance, as a newly single father, I used to be sloppy about my environment. I would go to bed, throw my clothes on the floor, get up, and leave them there with the bed unmade. Then I started to feel a little claustrophobic seeing the piles of stuff around constantly. So I began to pick them up, put them away, and even make the bed. I noticed something I wasn't expecting: When I took care of those things properly and neatly, it gave me a sense of satisfaction, even dignity.

So I started to take an interest in other aspects of the house. I developed more of a relationship with it, paying attention to the color combinations, the flow of light, and the sensory impressions I had in moving from room to room. I made more changes, and gradually my little old house was transformed. Of course this butted up against my daughter's pattern, but my point here is that this mindfulness then carried into every aspect of my life.

You can be mindful in many of the different tasks that you do. Think of it as having a quiet observer hovering over your shoulder, When you're walking, for instance, that observer helps you be mindful of the rhythm, pace, and tempo of your body. When driving, pay attention to the process of driving, the passing landscape, and the ongoing adjustments that you make as you drive. Or, when eating, slow down and be aware of your chewing and of the tastes and flavors. The first time I tried mindful eating I ate at a fraction of my normal pace. I noticed how I chewed, where I placed the food, and how my taste buds reacted. I was amazed at the explosion of exquisite tastes and sensations—and it was just a raisin! After something like that happens, it's easy to imagine all the other the things you miss in your life because your mind is so busy and so quickly moves on to the next thing.

So, slow down and take a few minutes each day to do mindfully whatever you are doing—taking a shower, listening to music, cooking a meal... *Learn to take interest in your world.* You might be surprised at the things you will find and appreciate that you haven't noticed before. As you do, your mindfulness gradually expands to the point where you feel more in tune with yourself and whatever is going on around you.

Exercise 20: Walking with mindfulness

You can learn to develop mindfulness in any of your daily activities —taking a shower, eating, driving, or so on. In this exercise, focus on walking.

1. In the beginning, identify a path or a route to take. This could be on your way to work, around the neighborhood, or a trail in nature.

2. Begin walking at a relaxed pace without fixing your eyes on anything, and bring your attention to your body. Be aware of each step you take, and while taking steps, pay attention to the movement

of your feet as they rise off the ground, move through the air, and come to the ground again.

3. With the awareness of the movement of your feet in the background as an anchor for your wandering mind, gently note the passing sights, sounds, smells—a breeze, a bird, the din of traffic, and so on. Just be generally aware as you walk. Experiment with seeing yourself from a distance as you walk, like an independent observer would see.

4. Walking mindfulness may be practiced in a number of ways with different degrees of concentration. You may want to try walking at slightly different speeds until you find a pace most suitable for you. With enough practice, you might find yourself walking mindfully wherever you go.

4
Follow Your Bliss

Don't ask so much what the world needs.
Go out and do what makes you come alive,
because what the world needs most
are people who have come alive.

—Howard Thurman

It's been nearly a half century since mythologist Joseph Campbell coined the phrase *follow your bliss* to teach the profound lesson of tapping into the energy that makes you tick. Following your bliss doesn't mean searching for anything that's not immediately available. It simply means to turn to that spark within you that knows in each moment what you want and what is best for you, and then following that. There is no clearer way to ride the positive energy of your greater spirit. To quote English jurist Michael Nolan, "There are many things in life that will catch your eye but only a few will catch your heart—pursue those." Why? Because your odds of success are greatly increased when you put your time and energy towards things that matter most—the things that represent the highest, most authentic part of you.

How much of your life goes into pursuing endless lists of desires, plans, and "ought-to-dos"? Do you ever question them? How much of what you think you want is what you've been conditioned to want? Is your mind full of thoughts about what you should do or are obligated to do? Do you ever ask or pay attention to what you are truly motivated to do? So many of us just follow the script, thinking we are free; but in reality, we are trapped.

The way out of this trap starts with taking time to become aware of your most heartfelt desires. Then you begin to simply follow them. You start with small steps. Then more and more you just follow wherever they take you.

The thought of what appears to be putting our own passions above commitments and responsibilities to our families, parents, lovers, clients, employers, and communities is quite scary to many of us. But the truth is that if you are truly committed to something you love, that is reflected back to you in the relationships, events, and circumstances of your life. Choosing to *follow your bliss* is probably the most unselfish act you can do, because it's impossible to be happy alone. When you *follow your bliss*, it gives you joy and satisfaction, and that dissolves your self-concern, opens you to others, and lets your basic goodness shine through.

I had a student, for instance, who faced a career choice between banking and consulting for a small start-up business. He really wanted the consulting option, but his parents thought that was too risky and would take time away from them. Their concern produced tension in the family. He chose to pursue his passion and—even though he was extremely busy—his resentments about their lack of support soon dissolved, and he made more time for them than ever. Hard to believe, maybe—until you experience it for yourself.

For most of us, following our bliss typically starts with making conscious choices about our careers and the kind of work that we do. Many struggle to find their calling, and those who do find it are still guaranteed to make mistakes before getting it right. You may never get it completely right, but you can get closer.

It's worth the effort to try. Satisfying work is one of the true pleasures of life.

Play to your strengths

Mihaly Csikszentmihaly, when he was a psychologist at the University of Chicago, discovered the concept of *Flow* in his study of high performance in sports, arts, and business. He describes *Flow* as a total immersion in a highly rewarding activity where the sense of self disappears. This immersion occurs where the activity provides a particularly meaningful challenge that is closely matched with your natural talents.

We all want to be good at something and to use our special talents—the innate abilities that just come naturally to us. These are different from skills and knowledge that we acquire. We do them without even trying, and they are what we enjoy doing most. When you are in your Flow, you are so immersed in exercising your natural talents that the sense of "work" disappears.

> Finding ways to apply and develop your talents through challenging tasks is a powerful source of self-worth.

Finding opportunities to apply these talents, and develop them through taking on challenging tasks, is a powerful source of self-worth, and in turn for achieving happiness and success. Playing to your strengths builds confidence and helps you become secure in your own uniqueness.

Many of us, however, *default our life choices to our learned ambitions rather than our innate abilities*. In that bargain, we expend a great deal of energy going against our own grain and doing things that don't come naturally to us. Worse, we are too quick to focus on improving what we are not so good at—and that can be deadening. No matter how hard you try, it's unlikely you will ever be more than average in areas where you don't have an aptitude. You are more likely to undermine your self-esteem by focusing too much on what you lack.

How different might it be to *follow your bliss* and use your natural talents? I have found that one of the more effective mental models in leadership is the simple rule of *play to your strengths, and manage around your weaknesses*. If you are a baseball player, for instance, you use your dominant hand to throw (play to your strength), and you use your other hand to catch (manage around your weakness) with the help of a glove, a tool.

Highly successful entrepreneurs, scientists, athletes, and artists achieve greatness by focusing on their strengths, not by developing their weaknesses. Tiger Woods, Bruce Springsteen, and Warren Buffet did not become great by working on their weaknesses. They discovered their talents at an early age and used, applied, and practiced them. My bet is that if you learn to be superb at something by playing to your strengths, you'll be happier.

If you're like me, though, you may not even be aware of your natural talents—you may have to discover them. In that case, you need to look within to find the gift that's yours to tap into. So pay attention to when you're at your best. When and where in your life do you feel most yourself and at the top of your game? What activities bring you the most joy? What are you doing when time just flies by? These are likely to be the areas of your natural talent and greatest potential.

A number of years ago, I came across an ancient framework for identifying natural talents and strengths that I found very compelling. I use it now in all of my leadership programs. This framework came from the study of indigenous cultures from across the world—Native American, African, Celtic, and Tibetan—that showed unmistakable similarities in their views of what it takes to be an effective human being. These cultures typically portray these views as four or five archetypal intelligences, laid out in the cardinal directions of the compass. Commonly known as a Mandala, or Medicine Wheel, this framework has withstood the test of time for thousands of years as a guide for personal growth and effectiveness.

Each of the directions represents a particular intelligence, a set of natural talents, for relating to the world and living in harmony with all things. Taken as a whole, they symbolize perfection and balance. The notion is that as you come into this world, you are born into a single direction, and so enter the world dominated by your root archetype. Yet the purpose of life is to seek self-understanding and completeness by learning to better access the other directions in becoming a more effective human being. I adopted a version of it in my book, *The Leadership Wheel: Five Steps for Achieving Individual and Organizational Greatness*.

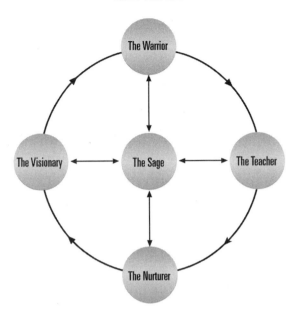

In describing the talents and strengths of the five intelligences, I always start in the direction of the East and the intellectual intelligence of the *Teacher*. If you are a Teacher you are inquisitive, rational, objective, analytical, fact-finding, and detail-oriented. These are the natural skills you call upon in trying to solve problems and understand the world. You like concrete things, see reality clearly, and suffer few illusions.

In the South is the emotional intelligence of the *Nurturer*. This is your feeling response to the intellect—or your heart response to your head. A Nurturer is a people person, and socially skilled—a good listener, communicator, networker, and team player. If you are a Nurturer, you focus on developing strong families, friendships, communities, teams, and cultures, and helping others become the best they can be.

In the West is the intuitive intelligence of the Visionary. If you are a *Visionary*, you take in the intellectual and emotional impressions of the first two directions, connect the dots, and make a plan for moving forward. You are a creative, conceptual, strategic, and systemic thinker, constantly seeking alternatives and new possibilities. You have insight and are able to see what matters most.

In the North is the action-intelligence of the *Warrior*. This is action in the sense that you see the plan emerging from the previous directions and make it happen. You are a task-oriented, risk-taking, tough-minded, and decisive person who can take charge, go after a challenge, and do what needs doing. You are also self-sacrificing in getting results because you do it for the greater good.

Finally, in the center, is the spiritual intelligence of the *Sage*. The Sage is the constant urge in us to learn, grow, and develop. It is subtly different than the other intelligences in the sense that *it is the hub that has access to the other intelligences and makes the Wheel turn*. If you possess Sage qualities, your predisposition to be aware, reflect, and be fully conscious makes you optimistic, empowered, and a fast learner. You are calm, serene, and open because your reflective quality enables you to adapt possibilities to conditions and conditions to possibilities, and make situations workable. This book focuses primarily on working with this intelligence.

Exercise 21:

> To identify and assess your natural talents and strengths, and to understand some of your potential weaknesses, please try *The Leadership Wheel* self-assessment exercise in the appendix on page 159. If you are really interested in learning more, my book develops those ideas in detail.

> Your talents do not necessarily channel into specific careers—people with the same or similar talents can be successful in different fields.
>
> •

In assessing your talents, however, you should know that they do not necessarily channel into specific careers. People with the same or similar talents can be successful in different fields. As a general rule, *you will be most successful when you craft your particular professional role to play to your strengths*.

I knew a VP for Human Resources, for instance, who was more of a data person (*Teacher*) than a people person (*Nurturer*). He was successful because he focused on building the data and analysis systems necessary to support colleagues with people skills on the front lines effectively. I also have a friend who was an investment banker and more of a people person (*Nurturer*) than an analyst or a hard-nosed negotiator (*Teacher-Warrior*). I asked, "How does that work? He said, "If you think about it, it's all about making a deal—people need to trust you." He played to his Nurturer strength.

This is equally true for my own career. At one point I was an assistant university comptroller in charge of producing quarterly and annual financial reports. I'm not very good at managing detail, and I had a real problem getting the rows and columns of the reports to add up, no matter how hard I tried! To make matters worse, my boss could smell a mathematical error as soon as it walked in the door. I was worried—it was a *Teacher's* job, and I was more of a *Visionary-Nurturer*. At about that time, however, the first spreadsheet software appeared on the market. So I put the numbers into the program, treated them like a system—my strength as a *Visionary*—and I was fine. Soon, nearly all of the financial reports from across campus were being generated from a spreadsheet.

So in this sense, career choice is first about knowing your strengths, and then about playing to them through the opportunities life presents. As Aristotle said, "Where your talents cross with the needs of the world, there lies your vocation." There are many ways to apply your talents.

This does not mean, however, that you can ignore your weaknesses. The basic strategy is still to *play to your strengths and manage around your weaknesses.* The fundamental message of The Wheel is one of balance. You probably will never turn a weakness into a strength because that's going too much against the grain. On the other hand, you still need to learn to manage your weaknesses well enough so they don't get you into trouble. In doing so, you learn to work all the directions of The Wheel, and as a result, become more balanced, more effective, and more happy.

Serve your purpose

Again I ask: Do you want a job (a teacher who thinks they just teach history), a career (a teacher who thinks they're in the business of education) or a calling (a teacher who thinks they're teaching young minds how they can make history)? If you have a purpose, you can see the difference. Likewise are you a brand manager for a pharmaceutical company, or a servant to public health? Are you a hairdresser or a counselor? Are you a banker, or a servant to community development? How are you framing or sculpting your career choice? Can you see that higher purpose to serve in what you do?

Once you begin to discover your talents, the next thing is to ask how you can use them in ways that give you meaning. What is your goal for your talents? Life goals usually center on work, relationships, and spirituality. But not all goals are equal. High achievement in work rarely makes someone as happy as high attainment in family, community, or spirituality. But fruitful, satisfying work can help make all the others more possible. When it comes to choosing work goals, then, the challenge is to choose something that matters to you—a purpose you want to serve.

Purpose helps you transcend the distractions of me-oriented pursuits and focus on something greater, more uplifting, and inspiring. It directs and guides you to make conscious choices in your decisions, instead of simply defaulting to the script. It also motivates and inspires you especially in the tough times. Finally, it taps into who you are deep inside—your beliefs, values, and passions for living. It reflects the authentic you, and in that is your source of power, magic, and influence.

> Purpose helps you transcend me-oriented pursuits and focus on something greater, more uplifting, and inspiring.

Finding a purpose to serve is not easy because it must be heartfelt and based on a personal truth. This means that it must be grounded in what is real for you and not an invented picture, and like your talents, it must be discovered. As Viktor Frankl said, "We do not invent our missions in life, we detect them." Detecting it is a process that calls on you to constantly ask who you are and what you care about. The "real you" revolves around this question.

There's no simple answer to that question; but often just living with it, without having a clear answer, is enough to motivate and guide you in the right direction. It is an age old question that all our world traditions have dealt with and they all say in one way or another the answer is to express our humanity fully—our basic goodness. Career choice is simply an aspect of that fundamental question. So what is it for you?

Try answering this question for yourself. Ask what is my true purpose in life? Or, who am I? as in Exercise 10 (page 46). Either question will do. Write down any response that pops into your head, a phrase is fine, and keep at it until you write one that tugs at your heart. You may write a hundred answers that don't stick, but when one starts to pull on your heart, you know you are onto something; it reflects your basic goodness. That's your purpose for now. Repeat this process periodically, and as you grow your purpose will grow. Eventually your destiny will discover you—your questions and your intention will draw it to you.

Early in my career, I often asked myself what I was called to do. Here, the book *Siddhartha* by Herman Hesse was a big influence on me. *Siddhartha* is an allegorical story that follows the spiritual journey of an Indian boy named Siddhartha during the time of the Buddha. His journey shows how happiness is attained not through scholastic methods, achievement, or pursuing the carnal pleasures of the world, but only through self-understanding. At one point, Siddhartha meets Vasudeva, a ferryman who has attained enlightenment by listening to the river. He is a deeply peaceful and happy man. "Vasudeva" means one who dwells and shines in all things. Siddhartha asks him for transport across the river, but says he has no money. Vasudeva takes him across for free, saying that "everything comes back." Later Siddhartha meets Vasudeva again, attains enlightenment by gently listening to the constant flow of the river, and becomes a ferryman himself.

From my first reading of the book, I knew I wanted to be some type of ferryman—one who guides people to the other side . . . from the old to the new. For me, this meant becoming a teacher of some sort but had no idea of what. In each step of my own journey, however, I took time to learn more about what gave me greatest meaning. In my case that's been learning how to make myself a better person in the process of helping others become more of who they most want to be.

I studied great literature, philosophy, and religion, practiced different styles of meditation and contemplative prayer, attended workshops on how to make work life better and people and organizations more effective . . . and did my best to practice what I had learned in whatever professional role I had. I was just playing to my strengths and interests. One thing led to another and eventually my destiny came to me in the form of being a coach and a facilitator of leadership—a ferryman. My avocation and vocation had become one and the same. All the study and work I had done drew it to me. Today, my purpose statement reads, "I use my coaching and facilitating skills to awaken everyone to their inherent basic goodness and inspire them to be that in the world."

What I find especially interesting about this process is that, when you

> When you detect your purpose, you will likely find that you want to do good in the world.

detect your purpose, you will likely find that you want to do good in the world. This is an expression of your basic goodness. I have helped thousands of students and professionals develop their purpose statements. Almost without fail, people want to make a positive impact on lives of others and the world—from "teach others biology to raise consciousness of planetary health" to "finance the development of stronger communities" to "use my humor and quick wit to bring joy to the workplace."

In his purpose statement one of my students wrote, "I will work for the success and betterment of myself, my family, my community, my nation, and my world. I will wake up every day wondering how I can do this. I will work hard to learn as much as I can, because with knowledge and understanding comes influence and strength. I will stay true to my beliefs. Along the way, I will make fulfilling and long-lasting relationships. Looking back on life, I will be proud of what I've done, who I've spent time with, and how I've spent my time. If I have achieved this, I have achieved success."

If he maintains that sense of purpose, I bet his chances of success, as well as happiness, are pretty good. I also wonder whether we would still suffer through the same old cycles of periodic economic upheaval if all our business leaders had such a purpose.

Exercise 22: Discovering your purpose

I borrowed this exercise from leadership guru Ken Blanchard, who has been an advisor and mentor to me in my professional life. He introduced this exercise at a workshop I attended. It is a very simple and elegant way to help identify purposeful potential. (Permission/ credit details are on page 4)

1. List some personal characteristics you feel great about. Use nouns. Examples: energy, courage, strength, enthusiasm, creativity
   I have _____

2. List ways you successfully interact with people. This time use verbs. Examples: teach, serve, lead, support, inspire, motivate
   I can _____

3. Visualize what your perfect world looks like. What are the people doing and saying? Write a description of this perfect world.
   My perfect world _____

4. Combine two of your nouns, two of your verbs, and your definition of your perfect world.
   My life purpose is _____

As I went through this exercise, I ended up with: "I use my coaching and facilitating skills to awaken everyone to their basic goodness and inspire them to be that in the world."

Craft the work you do to you until you find work you love (or come close)

The final step is to craft your work to you by playing to your talents and purpose in your work until you find new work that you love more. It's a journey. As Peter Drucker said, "The chances that the first career choice you make is the right one for you is roughly one in a million. If you decide the first one is right for you, then the chances are you are just plain lazy." It's just not likely that you will know your calling early in your career. However, if you play to your talents and your purpose, you will likely do well, and that will create new opportunities for you. Then you just continue to *follow your bliss* until you are led to it, or come close.

Picking up where I left off before about my own career, it took a few years for my calling to become clear. What I learned through the process, of course, was to *follow my bliss*. I kept asking questions, and my natural talents, interests, and sense of purpose showed me the way. Being lost at the end of the first part of my professional life, I wanted work that was more mission-driven. So I bailed out on sales and went into higher education, beginning in financial services. Why financial services? Again, I just needed a job. Playing to my strengths, I soon found an opportunity to design and implement financial reporting systems. That led to managing other kinds of change efforts, including facilitating strategic planning processes that helped people and organizations become more effective.

Suddenly everything came together. I began to see an opportunity to be a ferryman (my purpose) by helping to make organizations, and especially people, more effective. I found my calling simply by asking questions and following my talents, interests, and emerging purpose.

The fundamental message, then, is that any work you do in your life is a vehicle for waking up—whatever you have, that's it. Most career progressions only make sense in retrospect. There are probably multiple talents and places to exercise them as well as multiple purposes that you could serve authentically; but for the most part, the work you choose will depend on the circumstances and opportunities your life presents. Then *shape your job to you and not the other way around*. Even in the most routine things, you can exert some control over the essence of your work.

When you do, it's like Confucius said, "Find work you love and you will never work another day in your life."

Exercise 23: Rejuvenating your work

1. Review your answers to Exercise 6 (page 39). What do you like and what don't you like about your job?
2. How can you reshape it to play to your strengths and serve your purpose?

Learn to learn

To find your true calling, however, it is essential to remain vigilant in asking questions and paying attention to what gives you meaning. Be a conscious learner of what gives and does not give you meaning in work. I ask people not only to write mission statements, but also to pull them out every once in a while to ask how they're doing in modeling it and playing to their strengths. This often serves as a stimulus to make changes, and it is another reason why a space for daily reflection is so important. In being prepared, you will be in a position to take advantage of new opportunities as they arise. Highly effective people are able to get the most out of any situation because they constantly ask themselves how they are doing and what they want. They are learners who constantly seek and reinvent their ideal.

Exercise 24: Your ideal job

Using the journaling technique (Exercise 19, page 74), answer the following questions.

1. My ideal job description is . . .
2. My unique contribution to that job is . . .
3. The work that will make my grandchildren most proud is . . .

When in doubt, return to your purpose

Finally, when you're in a tough situation, or facing a difficult decision, go back to your purpose. You will always have bumps along the road. So, when in doubt, ask, "How do I serve my purpose in this situation?" How does this situation provide an opportunity for you to serve your purpose?

This purpose, of course, is an expression of your basic goodness—what is right, virtuous, and compassionate about being a human being. In serving it, you serve yourself and your growth. Guaranteed. In your career choices or in the business world in general, you are constantly faced with opportunities and decisions for which there are no clear answers. If you are faced with a new opportunity, and the road is not clear, draw on your purpose for guidance. If you are faced with an ethical dilemma, a sticky problem with another person, or at odds with your boss and uncertain what to do, ask, "How do I serve my purpose?" The answer typically becomes clear, and you can act with confidence, authenticity, and courage. There's a lot of power in that.

In the early years of developing the leadership fellows program at the university, I was embroiled in an intense debate around the strategic intent and operating philosophy of the program. Is this program about attracting the best and the brightest and placing them in the sexiest jobs, or is it about attracting those with the most leadership potential? Is leadership about building skills for success, or is it about making positive contributions? Is it about marching up the corporate ladder, or is it about service and responsibility? Is this just a scholarship program or can leadership actually be learned? "We don't want tree huggers!" was one of the common refrains.

I had an advisory group guiding the program that met regularly, and those meetings were by far the most passionate I have ever participated in—some might even say they were just downright rude! We could *not* arrive at consensus. Of course, as usually happens when that's the case, then my role and my philosophy as director of the program became part of the debate. I felt at risk.

At that point, I had a choice: give in, compromise, or stand by what I believed in. Of course by that time I had a purpose statement. I decided to just serve it and let the chips fall where they may. I may find myself out of a job, but I wouldn't be happy in that job anyway without doing what I believed in. To make a long story short, I quietly stood my ground, I'm still here, and I'm very proud of the program we have built. But without the clarity and conviction of my purpose, I doubt it would have turned out the same way.

So, in tough situations, simply frame your choices in terms of the purpose you serve . . . and follow where that takes you. It will be okay if you find yourself alone. And you may find yourself just where you want to be.

Either way, you find yourself.

5
Treat People as People

"We understand ourselves only through our relationships with others."

—Carl Jung

WHETHER YOU LISTEN to positive psychologist Martin Seligman or emotional intelligence guru Daniel Goleman, happy and highly effective people have rich, trusting relationships. Having others to share the ups and downs of life's experiences with intensifies the meaning of the experience, deepens the lessons and insights about ourselves and others that we gain from them, and celebrates our feelings of belonging, both personally and professionally. Abraham Maslow even argued that this sense for belonging must be satisfied before self-esteem and self-actualization can be realized. It is central to our greater spirit and evolutionary instinct—we seek friendship and social connection and resist their break-up or dissolution.

But what constitutes a good relationship? Is it getting along harmoniously, being loving, truthful, honest, supportive? These are certainly virtues and ideals that many strive for. Yet despite our efforts to do and be these things, we continually suffer in relationships. Why? Because your *relationships with others are only as good as the relationship you have with yourself.*

When you are unaware of your mental models, boxes, trips, issues, or whatever, you project them onto others, and relate to the others from a self-centered world. You objectify them, and it causes problems. You have your view, which is partial, and you project that view onto them without ever opening to theirs. Then you try to persuade them to that view, and if that doesn't work, then you find ways either to cope or leave.

Dealing with difficulties in relationship is very tricky. Even if you go someplace and learn effective communication skills, you are likely to "weaponize" those skills as tools to get your way. And that can just make things worse. People really can tell when you're trying to manipulate them—especially when you can't tell that's what you're doing.

When you are in a difficult conversation, for instance, ask yourself, "Am I trying to make this person wrong, or am I simply disagreeing with them?" Am I in here to just win or to listen to them first? There is an important yet subtle difference. In spite of the new skills you have learned, you still see others in terms of their relationship to your view rather than as they are in their own right. Your interactions with them are inauthentic, because you are still objectifying them. "They are not as busy as I am," or "This person doesn't help me."

As you *follow your bliss* and begin to discover your authentic self, worth, or purpose, you need to learn how to express your thoughts and feelings skillfully. Why? Authenticity begins with having the courage to speak and live your dreams publicly, and to respond to others and the situation in ways that honor your beliefs and values—particularly in challenging domains. Yet, as we are all inherently unique, expressing our authentic view inevitably leads to differences, and the differences lend themselves to difficult conversations. How you express your authentic self in such a situation is your key to establishing credibility, influence, and personal power. So how are you to do it effectively?

It's important to be honest, but being honest is sometimes tough. Reflect, for example, on the last time someone close to you asked you what's wrong, and you had difficulty being truthful. Rather than to confront the problem, did you make nice, not say anything, and just continue to feel hurt, guilty, or angry?

When you don't say what you are feeling, you create disharmony in your relationship. As philosopher Martin Buber said, "The origin of all conflict is that I don't say what I mean and don't do what I say." On the other hand, if you do say what you mean, it often comes across as disrespectful. So you're damned if you do and damned if you don't.

The question, then, is how can you be authentic without being a jerk? Being authentic is not just saying what's on your mind, it's also about expressing your truth in a way that honors both yourself and the other. It's okay to say "I'm irritated," for example, but not, "You're a jerk." It requires opening to others genuinely, and in doing that we learn to empathize and touch our basic goodness.

> How can you be authentic without being a jerk?
>
> •

Here are some keys.

Honor the "Thou"

One time when Martin Buber was praying, a graduate student knocked on his door and asked, "Can I see you?" Buber said, "Come back later." The student, who was depressed and struggling to find meaning in life, never returned. A little later Buber learned that the student had taken his life. This troubled him deeply and put him in a deep reflective mode as he wondered how he might have worked with this student differently. "Here I had a chance to be with God," he thought, "and I lost God in prayer." His reflections resulted in his most famous work, *I and Thou.* In it he argued that he had treated this student as an *It*—an object he wanted to go away—as opposed to a *Thou,* another child of God. The difference is profound.

So the first key is to *honor the Thou,* or as I learned from the Arbinger Institute, just *treat people as people.* When we treat others like an *It*, we objectify them—they either have what we want, are in the way of what we want, or are irrelevant to what we want. When they have what we want or are in the way of what we want, we make them blameworthy and become resistant to them. They sense it and respond in kind. Whatever underlying attitude you have, no matter how subtle, your partner will pick up on it and mirror it in return, and you end up never understanding each other.

The hard truth is that you can only change your relationships by changing your attitudes, not your behaviors. As William James said, "Whenever you're in conflict with someone, there is one factor that can make the difference between damaging your relationship and deepening it. That factor is attitude."

> When you treat people as people, you unhook yourself from this objectifying dynamic by seeing them as equal to yourself.
>
> •

If, for instance, you just *treat people as people,* you unhook yourself from this objectifying dynamic by seeing them as equal to yourself. It makes more authentic relating possible because it comes from the heart and not from your self-centered universe. As a result, your resistance to their presence drops, you connect to them, and you communicate. They sense it, and mirror it in return.

Exercise 25: How you treat others

1. Rate the key relationships in your life on scale of 1–10 according to how you treat the other person—with 10 meaning you treat them as a person and 1 meaning you treat them as an object.

2. Does the pattern look like the more you care, the less you objectify them?

3. For one week, whatever you do, try to benefit those whom you objectify most.

4. How does that change the relationship?

How do you do this? The first tip is, as friend once told me, *"If you want to be interesting, be interested."* You can't be intimate with others unless you can drop your self-absorption long enough to be open and take genuine interest in them. There is nothing more interesting to another person than your taking an interest in their favorite subject—them! As leadership guru Warren Bennis says, "I don't care how much you know, I want to know how much you care." So ask questions, probe, and listen. Do it sincerely.

Really listening, however, can be really difficult. Even when you think you are listening, most of the time you're just reloading your opinions, prejudices, and impulses, waiting for your next shot at getting them across. You can only truly listen when you are attentive and quiet inside. This opens you and helps you empathize with the other person. When you do really empathize, you touch your basic goodness.

Empathizing doesn't mean agreeing, necessarily; but when you empathize, the other person feels heard. Even better, if you really listen, the other person will likely listen in return, and you may both learn and be rewarded. Truly listening is a gift of understanding.

Exercise 26: Listening

Try this with a friend.

1. Take turns describing your favorite vacation ever while your partner acts as the worst listener you have ever experienced—distracted, interrupting, and so on. How does that feel?
2. Now describe something you have done really well while your partner really listens. Then change roles and listen to your partner describe something he or she has done really well.
3. In listening, try to absorb what your partner is saying. Catch the essence of it. Once you've done that, and actually feel that it's something they are or can be proud of, say something like, "So that was really something to be proud of!" How does that feel?

Listening becomes easier as you become more and more able to get out of your self-centered focus and focus your attention on the other person.

Take a minute and put yourself in their shoes. Better yet, imagine that you swap positions with them. What might they be feeling and thinking? What might it be like to be in relationship with you if you were them? How would that explain their behaviors? What might you do to help? Often this diffuses (or maybe de-fuses?) the tension and opens the heart. Also, consider the formative conditions that may have led to their particular point of view. If they simply don't know better, is that cause for your anger? What good does your anger serve in such a situation?

If those who are like wanton children
Are by nature prone to injure others,
What point is there in being angry—
Like resenting fire for its heat?

And if their faults are fleeting and contingent,
If living beings are by nature wholesome,
It's likewise senseless to resent them—
As well be angry at the sky for having clouds!

—Shantideva

When you step outside your self-centered boxes, you give others a different person to respond to; and in doing so, you change their world. Their interest and attitude begin to mirror yours. You enter a space where your understanding of one another expands and creates new possibilities for action. This doesn't mean you can't be angry or tough with one another. It just means honoring and respecting one another in doing so.

Exercise 27: Reframing a difficult relationship

1. Think back to the difficult relationship you identified in Exercise 8 (page 42) and consider their problems.
2. Identify ways you have added to those problems.
3. Try really taking an interest in them and putting yourself in their shoes.
4. From their perspective, is there something you can do that would help them?
5. What is the benefit, or cost, to treating this person this way?

I had a colleague who was quick to criticize, regardless of the circumstance. Worse, she would do it publicly. She was highly capable and expected everyone to commit and perform to her level, and when they didn't she just let them have it. It was her way or the highway. This put everyone around her on the defensive and on guard. Eventually people began to resist and collude against her, and they started to return her criticism and negativity in kind. She began to feel paranoid, and the situation spiraled.

Her work was highly valued and made her not someone to just let go, so I was asked to help. I started by interviewing first her and then those around her to get the full picture. In the meantime, something interesting happened. As I was taking several weeks to interview everyone, people started to report that her behavior had made a remarkable change for the better. She knew I was watching, and also instinctively knew how to change her behavior—to *treat people as people* by acting with more respect, kindness, and understanding.

When I met with her after completing all the interviews, she acknowledged this. I told her that whatever she was doing to just keep it up and I would check back in three months with her and everyone else. By the time I returned, the situation had completely turned around. The atmosphere was more open, people were more upbeat, and she less dark and gloomy. As she changed, others mirrored her change and the department changed. Everyone was happier and working better together.

I wish all cases were so easy, but it's such a simple truth—just *treat people as people*. A change in attitude can bring great rewards, because others can help us learn, grow, and awaken. *In essence, they become our teachers.* We can learn to be grateful to those who give us problems.

Exercise 28: Working with regret

1. Think of three things you have done involving other people that you regret.
2. Consider how when you did them, you were acting out of self-interest.
3. Now make a list of people you blame, people who have done you wrong.
4. How were they acting out of self-interest?

Use dialogue

I want to return to the story about my daughter always leaving a mess. Of course, picking up is a common teenage issue but our dynamic went to another level. We would argue and rationalize our views, and when that didn't work, I tried making deals. I often went to bed before my children, so we agreed that as long as she picked up before she went to bed it was okay.

This lasted for few days before the pattern reappeared. So then I told her that if it continued to happen her stuff would disappear. Sure enough it did, and one morning she asked where her book bag was. I told her it was in a black plastic bag in the basement (150-year-old house and an "icky" place to go). She was so angry that she slammed both the basement and front doors behind her as she left for school.

That night she came home and went straight to her room without even a saying a word or casting a glance. The next morning, as I was about to leave, I was looking for my shoes. I asked, "Where are my shoes?" and she replied, "Dad, they're in a black plastic bag in the basement!"

The problem was that I had been making an assumption that was at the bottom of the entire dynamic and didn't ever really check out her truth, her story. I was trying to get my way, thinking she was just undisciplined. Yet she was a straight A student, captain of her hockey team, an all-state orchestra bass player, and I never adequately acknowledged her for her accomplishments. As a result, when we fought over her picking up after herself, she felt totally unappreciated and power-tripped by me. So she did it in return. I suffered, she suffered, and our relationship suffered.

In the end, I tried a process called *dialogue* that I was learning at the time through my work. I dropped my stuff long enough to ask, with genuine interest, what was really going on with her. I used non-blaming language to explain my view, asked her about hers, and listened to her openly without trying to get my way or lay my trip on her. And that was the key. Once I related to her authentically, and without an agenda, she opened up too. She said, "All you want to do is pick on me about this and you never say anything about all the really good things I do." That hurt. So I stopped thinking of her as some thing to deal with, learned to acknowledge her, and our whole relationship turned around.

Did she get better at picking up after herself? A little, after all she was just a teenager. But what I gained in return was priceless.

Dialogue comes from the Greek word *dia-logos*, which means to create two-way meaning. Buber and many others have said that another key to improving relationship is to *use dialogue*, particularly in dealing difficult issues. Dialogue in this sense has been practiced for thousands of years, from Plato and tribal councils of indigenous cultures down to today's Quaker meetings, self-help groups, and organizational-change strategists. Combined with the attitude of *honor the Thou,* the practice of dialogue helps us stop objectifying people by learning to hear their story.

When you run into trouble in relationship, it's usually because you come at others with a particular view, position, or desired outcome that you push. When you do this, the other person pushes back in return and you go back and forth without really listening to each other. It looks a like a ping pong game. In the dynamic with my daughter and me, it was more like an exchange of artillery.

Dialogue brings in a different element. It begins with suspending your judgment and letting go of your intended outcome long enough to hear the other person's story. The basic approach is to state your view simply, authentically, and without blaming language, inquire into the other person's view, and listen genuinely to what they say. In the process, you each lay out your thinking and feelings so you can go beyond either one person's understanding. It is a reflective conversation where you treat the other person as a person, use language that is not loaded, ask questions to explore issues safely and openly, and listen to each other.

> The basic approach is to state your view simply and authentically without blame while inquiring into theirs and genuinely listening.
>
> •

For example, instead of saying, "You don't care about keeping others informed!" ask, "When we don't know what is going on, we get nervous. Can you see that? What do you think?" In modifying your tone and language, you can both open up. In the process of going back and forth, you each begin to reveal your assumptions, views, attitudes, boxes, and so on. It can be totally disarming. Each person feels heard and, as I was with my daughter, you will be surprised at the movement that comes. In this way of relating, expectations are not colored by accusation and blame, but by compassion and openness.

Communicating in this way offers the highest leverage for creating positive change in difficult relationships or sensitive issues. There is a whole range of literature on dialogue with various approaches, but it all boils down to sharing and exploring one another's views in an open way with an attitude of mutual learning. Versions of it are used in giving feedback, managing conflict, negotiating deals, coaching, and so on.

Exercise 29: Using dialogue

The three keys for success are:

1. *Take a learning attitude.* In approaching a dialogue, it is important to first check your intent: Are you in this to win or to learn, to defend a particular position or to search for something greater? You may be fairly certain of your position, but for the sake of the dialogue it is important to suspend that certainty for a moment and at least allow for another possibility.

2. *Use neutral language.* In approaching a dialogue, especially one dealing with a difficult or sensitive issue, it is important to pay attention to the language you use. Making attributions and using loaded words like "You're insensitive to others" or "That was a dumb move" puts people on the defensive and provokes them to respond in kind. So state your views without blame or judgment.

3. *Acknowledge your emotions.* Reveal your emotions and why you are feeling them. Emotions are often the driver, and to not reveal them is inauthentic; but how you reveal them is important. For instance, it's okay to say you're angry but it's not okay to insult or become aggressive.

Then follow a simple process.

1. *State your view without blame.* Reveal your story. A simple formula I use is Situation-Behavior-Impact—Here is the situation, the behavior I observed, and the impact on me, the task, or others. You simply share your thinking and feeling that led you to where you are.

2. *Inquire into their view and listen without judgment.* Then ask for their story. "What's going on for you?" Listen without judgment or resistance and gently probe until you find out what's going on for them. Again, you are trying to reveal their thinking and feeling just as you have already done for yourself.

3. *Seek a solution.* Going back and forth until you reveal one another's full story is typically the hard part. Next you explore a solution by making requests or offering suggestions. Again, offer them in a way that is not off-putting and that invites further exploration.

Try it with someone you're having an issue with. Work with the smaller challenges you have first and then as you gain confidence with it, try the bigger ones. This takes courage but the relief and reward in actually doing it successfully are well worth the effort.

Embrace the beloved

In today's world, we objectify even our romantic partners. See if this sounds right: First you look for and choose a mate. Then you try it out. Once you've had a chance to settle in together, you find out more about your mate. If you still like what you see, you stay put. If you don't, you leave and scout around for another one. In other words, whether it works or not depends upon your ability to find or attract the right partner. And if it doesn't work, the common solution is to divorce and start all over again with a new and, it is hoped, better mate.

There are two problems with this approach. First there is a tremendous amount of pain involved in switching. The division of possessions, the impact on the children, and the dissolution of dreams can have a deeply scarring effect on the emotions of everyone involved. Second, there is no growth or learning. Without taking a deeper look at why the relationship failed or is failing, you are apt to carry the same reasons for failure into the next one, and repeat the pattern.

Not everyone divorces when the relationship becomes unsatisfying. Some stay in the relationship anyway. As we have already seen, this too can have deeply negative consequences. Those who gut it out by living with the constant tension or in a parallel relationship where they ignore each other and never connect because "it's the right thing to do," dry up inside. They cope through distracting themselves with work, food, alcohol, activity, acquisition, porn . . .

But there is a better way. The truth is we may meet multiple potential "soul mates" in our lifetime. So just like with our careers, it's not necessarily about finding the perfect fit, it's about cultivating the one you are in. That's where the potential for growth is.

Here is one way of looking at it.

A number of years back, before our divorce, my wife and I had an opportunity to attend a couples' workshop led by Harville Hendrix. Hendrix developed a theory on relationships, authored a book called *Getting the Love You Want,* and has had tremendous success in leading couples into conscious healthy relationships.

> We develop an unconscious composite image of the dominant adults in our life ... and that image serves as a blueprint for what we seek in a partner.
> •

His theory works much like what we have already talked about. He says that in growing up we are socialized and develop an unconscious composite image, or mental model, of the dominant adults in our life. This image then serves as the blueprint for what we seek and are attracted to in a partner. In part, this attraction is based on the unmet needs we still have with our grown-ups, and represents the unfulfilled part of ourselves we want to complete. We then project this image onto our lovers, whom we subconsciously hope will complete the part of our relationship with our parents that we somehow missed.

At first we experience this attraction as "chemistry" as the unconscious mind makes the choice for us; and if it's strong enough, we "fall in-love." I guess it's a version of "opposites attract"—nature's way of connecting us with the "perfect" partner. "Perfect" in the sense that the person you choose is perfectly unqualified for meeting your unmet needs, or for giving you the love you believe you want. Eventually the image fades, and you enter a power struggle as you begin to seek *from your partner* what you somehow missed *from your parents*; but the Catch-22 is that the person you've chosen is incapable of giving you that.

It is only at the point of the power struggle, however, that the opportunity for healing and growing into real love actually begins. The "in-love" phase is *supposed* to end. That's part of nature's design for making sure we continue to evolve and grow whole. It also provides the glue that holds you together long enough to do the work and the healing. Your romantic relationship is a vehicle for discovering a greater self, and deeper, more mature love.

How do you do this? With courage and commitment, you *honor the thou* and *use dialogue* to work through the power struggle. You begin to explore, understand, and mirror the needs and feelings of your partner. Mirroring is paraphrasing what your partner has to say and asking if you got it right. It helps stop the destructive patterns. When you mirror one another, you help each other see your boxes, trips, issues, or whatever. You also begin to validate your partner. Validating helps you both feel heard. This doesn't mean that you always agree, but it does mean you understand how you each feel and you both feel heard and understood.

In the process you grow more intimate, and that intimacy leads to a deeper and more satisfying relationship. The projections stop and you begin to see one another for who you really are. Eventually you move from needing to be validated to appreciating "being seen" by your partner. "Being seen" means you have empathy and can imagine what your partner is feeling. Everyone wants to be seen—it's very powerful to be seen and appreciated for who you really are. When you "see and feel seen," all the games stop, you feel your basic goodness, and you begin to connect and open to one another's requests to make adjustments in how you relate. Intimacy deepens, and with it, so does the sex.

This of course is just one way of looking at romantic relationships. The essential point is that most relationships eventually do run into trouble, and instead of moving on to find the perfect fit, it can be well worth making a courageous, full-hearted attempt to cultivate the one you're in. *Embrace the beloved,* you may both grow up a little together.

My relationship with my wife followed much of this pattern exactly.

After a relatively short courtship, we eloped to Hawaii and got married barefoot on the beach on Maui. We wrote our own vows, and planned a second wedding to share our joy with our families. We returned and settled into starting our lives together. We were fully "in-love" and felt we had a great match.

A few years and a couple of babies later, however, problems started to appear. Although we rarely fought, we gradually became more distant. With the pressures of early careers and young children, the luster of the relationship began to wear off. We didn't seem to one another to be the people we had married anymore. To her, I seemed aloof and controlled; to me, she seemed overly sensitive and unsure of herself, even strangely distant. We were a perfect composite of our experience with our parents. Neither of us was getting what we wanted, and the power struggle began.

Friends of ours told us great things about the Hendrix workshop, so we decided to try it out. Early in the workshop, we were led through answering a series of open-ended questions about our experiences growing up and the dominant adults in our life. We were then asked, who did these answers describe? To our amazement, it was clear it was the person we had married. She married someone who she thought had a strong sense of himself (she didn't) and I married someone who I thought was nurturing (I wasn't). We were attracted to the parts of each other that we somehow missed as children.

Later in the workshop, we were asked to close our eyes and were led through a visualization exercise. We were asked to imagine silently an animal, any one that popped into our mind that somehow represented our relationship. We were then asked to share that animal, and we both said raccoon. Somehow we had both came up with a raccoon even though there was nothing in our past that might explain how that might be. It was out of the blue, and to me, that was magical. How was it possible?

About nine months later, we went to the beach for a family vacation. On the return home we stopped and spent the night at a friend's house in another city. I was up early as usual, and then her dog started a big raucous outside. Our friend went outside to find out what it was. She returned and said her dog had just cornered and killed a raccoon. My wife got up with all the noise and I told her what had happened. I said, "I know what this means." She looked at me with a frightened face and said, "I have to leave." About a month later we were separated.

We both understood the meaning of the synchronicity but could not explain why. Sometimes you just know you know something without really understanding it intellectually. So we did not get to heal our respective wounds of abandonment and identity with one another. But you can only work out these deep issues through relationship, and as we shall see, I eventually did by learning to embrace the beloved.

Exercise 30: Re-inventing your relationship

Often we simply get into ruts in our relationship, so we need to act consciously to bring them back to life and help it grow. Making a regular date or practicing random acts of kindness with your partner can bring significant reward. Another thing you may try in helping your inspiration is to use the journaling technique again to answer the following questions.

1. To love you means . . .

2. To become more aware of your hopes and fears means . . .

3. To have more fun with you means . . .

4. To deepen our relationship means . . .

Develop your support team

Another way to engage the unfulfilled parts you want to complete is to build a community of support. Being somewhat reserved and distant by habit, and wanting to learn more about groups and facilitation, I felt a need to push myself in that direction. Knowing of my interest, a friend told me about M. Scott Peck's book, *The Different Drum*. It was a bestseller about developing intentional community. Peck begins the book with a wonderful fable called "The Rabbi's Gift" that intrigued me immediately. The following is a version of this story and its message is very similar to Buber's.

"The Rabbi's Gift" is a story about a monastery that had fallen upon hard times due to people's waning interest in things religious. Once a great order, it had dwindled over the years to the extent that there were only five monks left, the abbot and four others, all over seventy in age. Clearly it was a dying order.

A deep forest surrounded the monastery, and in it was a little hut that a wise old rabbi from a nearby town used for a hermitage. Through their many years of prayer the old monks could always sense when the rabbi was in his hermitage, and they often wondered about him. As he agonized over the future of his order, one day the abbot decided to visit the rabbi to ask for advice.

The rabbi welcomed the abbot to his hut but could only commiserate with him. "I know how it is," he exclaimed. "The spirit has gone out of the people. It is the same in my town. Almost no one comes to the synagogue anymore." So they wept and prayed together. When the abbot had to leave, they embraced each other and the abbot asked, "So is there nothing you can tell me, no piece of advice you can give me that would help me save my dying order?"

"No, I am sorry," the rabbi responded. "I have no advice to give. The only thing I can tell you is that the Messiah is one of you."

When the abbot returned to the monastery his fellow monks gathered around him to ask, "Well, what did the rabbi say?"

"He couldn't help," the abbot answered. "The only thing he did say, just as I was leaving, was that the Messiah is one of us; but I don't know what he meant."

In the days and weeks and months that followed, the old monks wondered whether there was any possible significance to the rabbi's words. The Messiah is one of us? Could he possibly have meant one of us monks here at the monastery? If that's the case, who? As they contemplated this question, the old monks began to treat each other with extraordinary respect on the off chance that one of them might be the Messiah. They saw the beauty and wisdom in the abbot as well as in brothers Thomas, Philip, and even crotchety old Eldrid!

Because the forest in which it was situated was beautiful, it so happened that people still occasionally came to visit the monastery to picnic on its tiny lawn. As they did so, they sensed the aura of extraordinary respect that now began to surround the five old monks and seemed to radiate out from them. There was something strangely attractive, even compelling, about it. Hardly knowing why, they began to come back to the monastery more frequently to picnic, to play, to pray. And they brought friends, and their friends brought their friends.

Then some of the younger men who came to visit started to talk more and more with the old monks. After a while, one asked if he could join them. Then another, and another. So within a few years the monastery had once again become a thriving order and, thanks to the rabbi's gift, a vibrant center of light and spirituality in the realm.

In reading this, I was so inspired by the idea of intentional community that I decided to try it. I wrote a letter inviting friends and acquaintances whom I thought might be interested. My thought was to bring a group of about sixteen people together every other week in one of our homes for a few hours for the purpose of developing a circle of friends and exploring life together. I asked them to come the first night if they were interested, or pass the invitation along to someone else if they were not. There would be no structure to the group.

In the letter I explained, "My hope is to form a circle of friends who can be supportive of one another in finding ways to do things we each love. I would like to like to learn from our differences, heal so we can become more open to exploring our journeys together, and care for one another with an understanding that we are all connected. Above all, I want to have fun."

The first night fourteen people showed up, only half of whom I knew. We experimented with different exercises and different venues, and we took turns designing and facilitating the group activities. We shared our histories, we acted out some of our life dramas, we gave one another feedback and support, we did spontaneous dances in silence, and in every instance we allowed everyone to share their heart's longing and grief in a place of acceptance and safety.

The group changed periodically, as a few dropped out and others joined in; but we continued to meet every other week for almost four years. It was life-affirming as well as life-changing for almost everyone. In many ways, we all grew up a little together in the process. We learned about ourselves, we learned how to be there for one another, and we learned how to get out of some of our boxes. I also developed a circle friendships, my support group, that continues to this day.

Honoring others and relating to them in an intimate way is essential to your well-being. Absent such opportunities, you can leave yourself feeling empty, lonely, and unaffirmed. When you are suffering from a problem at work or in a relationship, for instance, whom do you go to for advice and support? You can go to a bar and have drinks with your friends, but often that ends up in just drowning your sorrows in gossip and idle talk. Do you really have someone with whom you can truly open about your feelings, and who can genuinely empathize in return?

Intimate friends and family help you by serving as a reality check, offering new ideas and giving emotional support. They validate you and serve as mirrors in helping you learn about yourself. They also make you feel supported and not alone in dealing with the tough times.

And when a friend is in need, do they come to you? If not, perhaps that's a message for you. If so, and you are genuinely there for them, the interesting thing is that this too is wonderfully affirming. You feel good about yourself—it touches your basic goodness.

In both receiving and giving support, you see how you can discover a deeper sense of yourself, and a greater sense of belonging and significance. When you surround yourself with people who support you, your energy expands.

> In both receiving and giving support, you discover a deeper sense of yourself, and a greater sense of belonging and significance.
>
> •

So how do you develop a circle of intimacy? Many of you already have a group; but for those of you who do not, you can form or join a group that meets regularly. I have seen many people transformed through a book club, a poetry group, a men's group, a women's group, or what have you.

Even at work you can do this. I form coaching teams of three, for instance, in my workshops to have participants support one another in their development plans and professional challenges. Some of these coaching teams continue to meet for years afterwards. Several coaching teams made up of my former students continue to connect regularly even though the people in them are separated by time, distance, and career interests.

Networking is another way of developing a community of support at work. The value of professional networks is obvious, but in my experience, most people don't know how to build them effectively. Most know that it's important to join clubs, do lunches, mingle at conferences and socials, and so on to meet people; but many don't understand what to do when face to face with someone. They end up trying to sell themselves and then it just becomes another ping pong match. Remember, *if you want to be interesting, be interested.* If you take an interest in the other person by asking questions about what they do, what they enjoy, and so forth, you have a far better chance at developing a lasting connection. In learning to help and support, your network naturally manifests around you.

None of us travels through life alone. We've all been helped, influenced, and supported by others. Find your community to help you learn and keep you on track to achieve what you have committed to do.

Exercise 31: Develop your circle

1. Draw a circle on a piece of paper and write the names of people
   you are close to in it.
2. How have they contributed to your life?
3. How have you supported them?
4. What do you do to nurture the relationship?
5. What kinds of conversations do you have with them?
6. Do these need to change?
7. Who might you want to bring in closer?
8. Is there someone else you know whom you would like to bring
   into your circle?

Forgive with courage

I'd like to share an old tale from an unknown source.

There once were two brothers living on adjoining farms who fell
into conflict. It was the first serious rift in forty years of farming
side by side, sharing tools, and trading labor and goods as needed
without a hitch.

Then the long partnership fell apart. It began with a small mis-
understanding and grew into a major difference. Finally it exploded
into an exchange of bitter words followed by months of silence.

One morning there was a knock on the older brother's door. He
opened it to find a man looking for work. "I'm looking for a few
days' work," he said. "Perhaps you would have a few small jobs here
and there. Could I help you?"

"Yes," said the older brother. "I do have a job for you. Look across
the creek at that farm. That's my neighbor. In fact, it's my younger
brother. A few months ago there was a meadow between us, and then
he dug a trench and now there is a creek between us. Well, he may
have done this to spite me, but I'll go him one better. See that pile

of lumber curing by the barn? I want you to build me a fence—an eight-foot fence—so I won't need to see his place anymore. Cool him down, anyhow."

The man said, "I think I understand the situation. Show me the nails and tools and I'll be able to do a job that pleases you."

The older brother had to go to town for supplies, so he helped the man get the materials ready and then he was off for the day.

The man worked hard all that day measuring, sawing, nailing.

About sunset, when the farmer returned, the man had just finished his job. The farmer's eyes opened wide, and his jaw dropped.

There was no fence there at all. It was a bridge . . . a bridge stretching from one side of the creek to the other! A fine piece of work, handrails and all—and the neighbor, his younger brother, was approaching, beaming with tears in his eyes and his hands outstretched.

"You are quite something to build this bridge after all that's happened between us."

The two brothers stood at each end of the bridge, and then they met in the middle, taking each other's hand and hugging one another. They turned to see the man hoist his belongings on his shoulder. "No, wait! Stay a few days. I've a lot of other projects for you," said the older brother.

"I'd love to stay on," the man said, "but, I have many more bridges to build."

So what do you do when you feel wronged by another?

Most of the world's traditions teach about the power of forgiveness. Gandhi forgave his assassin while he lay dying. Earlier in his life he even said, "The weak can never forgive. Forgiveness is the attribute of the strong." Likewise Pope John Paul II forgave his would-be assassin while visiting him in prison. These were powerful, transformative acts. Today's research shows the same—people who forgive are happier and healthier.

Holding on to
the feelings of
resentment from
a perceived wrong
doesn't rectify the
offense, it only
causes stress.
•

Understanding why is not rocket science. Holding on to the feelings of resentment from a perceived wrong doesn't rectify the offense, it only causes stress. If someone badmouths you, for instance, your initial feelings of hurt fester and build up into anger and resentment. Your "spinning" may even lead you to start plotting your revenge to badmouth in return, but such negativity only breeds further negativity. What you put into the world comes back to you.

Forgiveness ends this pattern, and lets you experience the present free from the contamination of the past. It doesn't mean making the other person right or wrong, it simply means letting go. In the case of being badmouthed by another, it could mean letting go of your "trip" of needing to be respected by everybody, or of the resentment, or of making the other person wrong. For your own sake, be courageous enough to get off that righteousness. If you are convinced you are justified, then simply forgive the person but don't forget the act. The forgiveness is a gift to yourself for overcoming the hurt, bringing closure, and moving on.

But it isn't easy. Divorces, for instance, are often particularly difficult, and the lingering negativity, guilt, or anger can creep into other relationships, especially if there are children. So it's important for everyone's sake to let go and move on, but that takes time and deliberate effort.

When you do let go, there is an immediate release of tension in the heart. Have you ever forgiven, for instance, and noticed the sense of relief and openness in the heart? I have found a joyful, sad, loving feeling in it—my basic goodness shining through.

Exercise 32: Forgiving

Consider someone you have not forgiven or find difficulty forgiving. Perhaps it's one of the people you identified in Exercise 8 or 27.

1. Remember that forgiveness doesn't mean you approve or forget whatever happened. You forgive the doer, not the doing.

2. Also think about how you are the only person responsible for your feelings and for healing the hurt that is going on inside of you.

3. Finally, remember that you may have had some part in what happened. Be willing to face up to that part and accept it without blame.

4. Then, put yourself in the shoes of the person you feel wronged by. What was his or her life like at the time it happened?

5. You might try talking to the other person, because you may not be ready to forgive until you have shared your story and heard theirs. This is a courageous act on your part and it has nothing to do with whether the other person can admit they are wrong. You are forgiving to liberate yourself, no matter what the other person decides to do.

6
Work the Law of Cause and Effect

"God does not play dice."

—Albert Einstein

C AN YOU THINK of anything that exists independently of everything else? Is there ever a thing that isn't at least in part created by something else? A tree grows from a seed or a lake from drops of water or a fall season from the summer—this is the rhythm of nature. Every single object or event is created *only* in relationship to other objects or events. All is interdependent and constantly changing.

Have you ever had the feeling that there are no accidents in life? That everything happens for a reason? Neither success nor failure is an accident, or the result of good or bad luck. What happens is the result of series of specific choices and steps you have taken that bring you to where you are, and they could not have brought you to any other place.

If you look at the diverse lives of very successful people, whether they started off with certain advantages or not, you can see in their backgrounds a series of steps they took to their success. If you look at the lives of people who suffer from lack of money, problems in relationships, or unsatisfying work, there too you can trace their situation back to choices they made that caused it. Yes, circumstances are a factor, but the choices made relative to those circumstances are what make the most difference.

What I am pointing to here is the law of cause and effect. We've talked about it some already, but now I want to be more explicit about it. Plato was the first in the West to describe this law, and his thinking was the foundation for much of the philosophy and science that followed. In the East it is known as the law of karma, and it operates as the universal governing principle of the cosmos, without any exceptions. It cannot be escaped because nothing falls outside of its scope.

Every event or action is the result of interdependent causes, does not exist independently of those causes, and is itself a cause of other events or actions

•

This law is a law like gravity is a law—it's not one you can choose to break. Because of it, every event or action is the result of interdependent causes, does not exist independently of those causes, and is itself a cause of other events or actions. For every effect you experience, there is a cause, or a series of identifiable causes.

There are several aspects to this law. First, for every thought or action there is a reaction. If you drip water in a bowl, for instance, eventually it will fill with water. All your thoughts and actions have consequences. If you are moody, you can make others defensive. Your mind is a powerful force and can shape your reality. That is why successful people tend to be thoughtful and aware of what they do, while those who are less mindful get into trouble. If you act with awareness and a plan, you will bring about what you desire—it isn't just luck. I was successful in sales early in my career because I did all the right things to bring it about. It's pretty basic, but many of us never or only half-heartedly think and act this way.

Second, as the saying in the New Testament goes, "What you sow is what you reap." If you plant an apple seed, you get an apple and not something else. If you sow a good cause, you will reap a good benefit; but if you sow anger, you will reap resistance. What you put into the world, you get back.

If you are experiencing a repeated pattern in your life, you are probably doing something to cause it. More subtly, however, what you reap today is the result of what you have sown in the past. The results of your actions and thoughts are not necessarily immediate; they may take time to appear.

Finally, there are no accidents. The uncanny coincidence, the unlikely conjunction of events, or the startling serendipity—who hasn't had them happen in their life? You think of someone for the first time in years, and run into them a few hours later. You hear an unusual phrase, and then hear it three times in the same day. You are on a back street in a foreign country, and you bump into a college roommate. You are at a bookstore, a book falls off the shelf, and it's exactly what you need.

We've all had moments when things come together in an almost unbelievable coincidence that seems to help or guide us along our path. Carl Jung called these coincidences "synchronicity." In some subtle and usually imperceptible way, you have sown a cause that has attracted them to you.

Just being aware of this law of cause and effect will not produce any change in your life. Like any other principle, knowing about it will prove to be useless unless you apply it. It is part of the same energy field as your hungry spirit. Happy, healthy, successful people have learned to work it.

Here are some tips how.

Magnetize your intention

Everything you achieve in your life starts with a goal, an aspiration, or an intention. If you hold this intention strongly in your heart and mind, you will draw what you intend to you like a magnet. Why? Your intention or goal serves as a cause that taps into this universal law to bring about your desired result. Just like when you tend a seed, if you nurture your intention in a healthy, focused, and positive way, it must produce a result similar to that seed.

As I write this book for example, the world sends me messages to include from the nightly news, a conversation with a friend, a glance at an article. Why? My mind has that intention, is aware and looking for it to be realized, and attracts the responses. When you really want something, the whole world conspires to help you get it.

> When you really want something, the whole world conspires to help you get it.
>
> •

Athletes use this fact to enhance their performance. Through visualization, guided imagery, and mental rehearsal, they create a mental image or intention of what they want to happen, and performance improves. By imagining a scene, complete with images of their best performance or a desired outcome, they are instructed to simply "step into" the feeling at its core.

A popular although not verified story about this power is attributed to Vietnam War pilot Major James Nesmeth, who was shot down and held as a prisoner of war for seven years. After his release and rehabilitation, he played his first round of golf and cut nearly twenty strokes off his game. When asked how that was possible, he responded, "You have to do something in solitary confinement, otherwise you would go crazy. So I played a round a golf over and over again in my mind."

Your life purpose that you worked on in Exercise 22 (page 89) is an intention. If you hold it dear, and take the right steps to actualize it, you will eventually draw to yourself all that's needed to fulfill it. Sure, this may sound a little woo woo—but it works. As you get clearer on the details, you'll see.

I shared earlier the story of how this worked for me: I wanted to teach but instead of going back to school I just took little opportunities to teach and lead groups wherever I could. Eventually that led me to it. The interesting thing is that the process didn't work out exactly the way I expected. I am really more of a facilitator than a teacher, which I find more perfectly fits my original purpose. As Khalil Gibran said, "The teacher who is indeed wise does not bid you to enter the house of his wisdom but rather leads you to the threshold of your mind." That is more like what a ferryman does. In the end, you get what you need.

This also was true for other aspects of my life. I had always wanted, for instance, to have a spiritual teacher. I volunteered for Peace Corps with this hope in mind. Initially they wanted to send me to Africa and then to Micronesia, but I said no because I wanted to go to Asia where I thought I might find a teacher. We went back and forth for months. Then one day I received another letter from them and—Nepal! I attended my first meditation retreat there and for almost two decades afterwards I went on annual retreats led by different teachers. I met a lot of wonderful people, but never really connected with any of them.

Part of the reason I didn't was that meeting a spiritual teacher was still just a nice, romantic idea I had picked up from a book in my early twenties. But later, through the depths of my despair in midlife, my intention deepened. My heart was broken, and I felt a newfound commitment to really devote myself to a path of practice. Almost as soon as I made that commitment inwardly, I started meeting teachers with whom I felt genuinely connected. Within the span of few months, I met six teachers—including His Holiness the Dalai Lama. I went from nothing to unimaginable riches. As the saying goes, when the student is ready, the teacher appears.

Readiness is the key. Your intention must be pure as well as deep. If it's mixed with other things, the results will be mixed too. Likewise if it isn't sincere or heartfelt, then you won't invoke the magic. This is very important.

In the case of meeting my teachers, I had always had the intention, but it wasn't clear and I wasn't fully committed to it. It was an intellectual idea, and I wasn't willing to give up anything or put any skin in the game to get it. My intention was mixed, so the results I attracted were mixed. That changed, however, with all the turmoil in my life. As soon as I was committed (not to an asylum, thankfully), I got very clear and the results were almost immediate.

If your intention is mixed with fear or comes from a sense of lack, though, it may backfire. If you desire wealth because you feel a sense of poverty, for example, then you may get wealth; but it will be mixed with a bitter aftertaste like feeling too busy or stressed. Your intention must be pure, not "I want this because I feel I need it" but rather "I want it because I want it." In needs to be intrinsic, and as said before, that intrinsic quality for the most part must be detected and not invented. In other words, your intention needs to go beyond being a simple, nice idea that is invented out of thin air. Instead, it needs to be discovered and based on something deeper and more heartfelt.

Likewise if your intention is mixed with doubt, you will attract doubt. Not only people, but the universe itself, can sense a lack of commitment to a goal. Has someone ever told you about a goal of theirs, and you can just sense how wishy-washy and uncertain they are about it? They say things like, "Well, I'm going to try this and see how it goes. Hopefully it will work out okay." Is that evidence that a clear commitment has been made? Not remotely. Are you going to help this person? Probably not. On the other hand, if you feel committed, you will attract commitment.

So the intention must be pure and deep. To be so, it must be authentic—and as we have seen, what is most authentic comes from the basic goodness of greater spirit. Am I writing this book, for instance, to become rich and famous, or to make a contribution? If for the former, it might come across to you as so. I might make money, but I wouldn't be entirely believable and wouldn't have the impact I intend. How can I help you tell the difference? I'm hoping it comes across through my openness in the stories I share. If I hold back through fear of something, I expect that you also would hold back.

Here is a simple process:

First, get very clear on your intention—the more clarity the better. Remember: What we focus on we draw to us.

Second, believe in it, and believe that your thoughts shape your reality. If you don't think the intention can work, it probably won't. If you can't commit to your intention, you probably won't be able to attract it.

Third, let go of the how and the when. Once you've set an intention, it's time to let your trust and faith take their course. You should take steps but don't be too directive, or planful. Let the energy work its magic by allowing your intention to unfold in the perfect time, manner, and form. If you are too attached to a specific outcome, you cut off or restrict the natural flow. If your intention is pure, there is no way you can make a mistake.

Appreciate your world

Einstein used to ask, "Do you believe in a friendly Universe or a hostile Universe?" Your world in part reflects your attitude towards it. If you begin to look for the good in your life and in your world, you are likely to find it. Again, you can create your own reality. It works the same way as intention: You bring into your life whatever you focus on. If instead of thinking about what you don't have in your life, you think about what you do have, it makes a difference. If you really do believe that the world acts in your best interests and brings you what you need, then it's likely to work that way.

How many times have you heard of someone losing their job only to end up in a better place, or losing a spouse through divorce only to have their world open to them in an entirely different and positive way? Do you think it's an accident when that happens? I don't. When you appreciate yourself, others, and the world around you, and look for the good in things, good things happen in return. *Basic goodness magnetizes basic goodness.*

Have you ever noticed that when things go wrong in one aspect of your life, they tend to go wrong in all the other aspects, too? You may have problems with your health, your job, and your relationships all at once. Better yet, have you known anyone whose life was constantly filled with drama? Why was it so? *My bet is their world is mirroring their frame of mind.* Again, it's about attitude. Charles Swindol wrote:

> The longer I live, the more I realize the impact of attitude on life. Attitude to me is more important than facts. It is more important than the past, than education, than money, than circumstances, than failures, than successes, than what other people think or say or do. It is more important than appearance, giftedness or skills. It will make or break a company . . . a church . . . a home . . . a person. The remarkable thing is, we have a choice every day regarding the attitude we will embrace for the day. We cannot change our past . . . We cannot change the fact that people will act in a certain way. We cannot change the inevitable. The only thing we can do is play on the strings we have, and that is our attitude . . . I am convinced that life is 10% what happens to me and 90% how I react to it. And so it is with you . . . we are in charge of our attitudes.

You saw how, when I doubted myself in midlife, I began having problems in every aspect of my life. I could only see what was wrong and my world treated me the same. But as soon as I rediscovered my basic goodness, regained my confidence, and began to appreciate what I had, my world immediately changed for the better. I found my dream job, published my first book, moved back into my old house, and met my spiritual teachers—all within a forty-five-day period! The forces of the Universe aligned to help me as soon as I came from a place of hope instead of fear.

> When I'm dark and full of doubt, my world is dark and full of doubt. But when I am light and full of hope, my world is light and full of hope.
> •

We get what we need if we look upon the world with hope and appreciation. It is an attitude, and it does open us to possibilities that make the world more workable for us. In our lives, there always is plenty to be grateful for; but if we focus on what's not going so well, we become tight and defensive and the world responds in kind. When I'm dark and full of doubt, my world is dark and full of doubt. But when I am light and full of hope, my world is light and full of hope.

It's like as a friend once asked me, "What do a frog's eyes see?"

"Well, I don't know, I answered. "What do they see?"

"Flies!"

His point was that a frog is wired to see flies almost to the exclusion of anything else. If we look upon the world with fear, we experience resignation but if we look on it with hope we see opportunity. This is an expression of the law of cause and effect—what we put into the world returns in kind. So to experience life as a gift, let go of your self-concern, appreciate what's around you, and practice looking at life as a gift.

Exercise 33: Appreciation activities

1. Before going to bed, think of what you can appreciate from the day—feelings, events, activities. How does that impact your thoughts about them?

2. Visit people who have contributed to your life and thank them, or name the strength of another person and call it out. How does it feel? How does it impact your relationship?

3. Think of a time in your life when something you thought was

bad happened but turned out to be beneficial. Look for more instances. Was the Universe working for you?

4. For a few moments, imagine that your death is just around the corner. How does that change your appreciation of your world?

Turn problems into opportunities

Quoting his teacher, anthropologist, author, and mystic Carlos Castaneda said, "The difference between an ordinary person and a warrior is that an ordinary person takes every problem as a burden and a curse whereas a warrior takes it on as a challenge and opportunity." So related to *appreciating your world* is to *turn problems into opportunities.*

Every day we face challenges. Usually we see them as problems, burdens, because the world is not conforming to our view—our box. These problems cause us enormous stress, frustration, and anxiety. Yet we can reframe them by changing our attitude and treating them as opportunities to learn and grow as a person.

For example, someone says something to you that's rude or offensive. Instead of seeing this as a problem situation, you can reframe it as an opportunity to practice patience and forgiveness, and to work skillfully with the other person. You can redirect the anger in a positive way. Then the rude person is actually a gift—a teacher for helping you grow.

If you only look at what's wrong, you'll only see problems. The more you focus on your issues the more you will attract what reinforces them and feel angry, victimized, and bitter. In contrast, if you look for solutions, for lessons to be learned and changes to be made, you'll begin to attract opportunities. If you are out of work, for instance, you might desperately start looking for another job. Alternatively, you might change your mental model by looking upon this as the opportunity to now do anything you want, get the *right* job, or start your own business.

How you respond to these challenges is often described as what makes the difference between being a victim and a victor. "My boss doesn't respect me," "I'm not paid enough to do that," "I just do what I'm told" are responses of a victim. You play the blame game—you blame the bureaucracy, the boss, the weather, the food. You can blame an infinite number of things, but when you do this, things get complicated. People start to blame back and it's ping pong again.

Instead of being a *victim* like this—where you remove yourself from having any part in making the situation as it is—you could choose to be a *victor*. You choose to be a victor by taking some of the responsibility for the situation on yourself, looking for the opportunities the situation presents, and working with them constructively. Being a victor doesn't always mean that you *win*, but it does mean choosing to see and play the game a different way.

Being a victim happens to all of us from time to time. The important point is to become aware of when it's happening, so you can turn it around. Again, it's about attitude, your mental frame.

Victim	Victor
Nothing I can do	I look at alternatives
It's the way I am	I choose another way
They make me mad	I control my feelings
They won't allow it	I can change it
I can't	I will
I have to	I prefer to
If only	What if

"My barn burned down, but hey, now I can see the moon at night!"

—Unknown

Exercise 34: From Victim to Victor

This exercise is a nice recap of many of the previous exercises. I like it because it underscores the importance of attitude in dealing with many of our problems.

First, think about a difficult situation, decision, or relationship you have been part of or are going through (ineffective meeting? career challenge? harsh conversation?) in which you played the victim.

1. What happened to you?
2. What was your attitude? Did you react and become defensive, cope, shut down, complain, or just go along with others?
3. What was the impact of your response? On you? On the other(s)?
4. How do you feel in the victim's place?

Now think about a difficult situation in which you played the victor —one where you learned, grew, or successfully met the challenge.

1. What problem did you face?
2. What was your attitude? How did you react in a positive way?
3. What was the impact of your response?
4. What inner resources, values, passions, and principles did you draw on to guide your actions?
5. How did it feel to be a victor?

All of us can easily fall into a victim mentality, but just being aware of when we do is often enough to pull us out of it.

Behave into new ways of being

Just like our thoughts, feelings, attitudes, and intentions, our actions are causes and have consequences. If you can't muster the feeling of confidence, then just act confidently until the feeling comes. In other words, when all else fails, *just do it*. Acting with confidence can build confidence.

Daniel Goleman says we don't think our way into new behaviors, we behave our way into new ways of thinking. Again, it's the law of cause and effect. We can rewire ourselves through our actions, and those actions can lead to changes in our being. To quote poet John Dryden, "We first make our habits, then our habits make us."

Philosopher William James once asked, "Do I sing because I am happy or am I happy because I sing?" Singing evokes happiness, even when we are feeling down. Instead of the power of positive thinking, it is the power of positive action. Similarly, acting with kindness evokes feelings of kindness, and expressing gratitude makes one feel grateful. It's the same principle.

It's the same with building self-esteem at work. Often I hear of people shying away from something because they don't feel fully prepared. I believe this is usually their self-doubt talking. Don't wait until you feel good enough or confident enough before taking on a big challenge—jump in and try it. It's not really about feeling good or prepared, it's about the quality of your effort. Do it, muddle through, experience failure, and learn on the way. Eventually you will begin to succeed.

Act, and the self-esteem will come. Try it and see what happens.

Exercise 35: Happiness triggers

1. Think back to your responses to Exercise 9 (page 45). What are some of the thoughts or activities that make you happiest?
2. When feeling down, bring these to mind or engage in them, and see what happens.

Give generously

A few years ago I arranged for students to do volunteer clean-up work for a local land trust. We spent the day cleaning up garbage that had been dumped on recently acquired property near family homes in a poor rural community. The day was wet but we had fun in the muck, mire, and stench of the clean-up. By the end of the day we were tired and dirty.

In our closing circle, I asked everyone for their personal reflections. As we went around the circle, everyone was expressing their gratitude and appreciation for the opportunity to help. Then we came to a student who was in tears. She said that the highlight of her day was when she went up to say hello to one of the families. They thanked her from the bottom of their hearts for cleaning up their "back yard." Now the children could play again in the forest without fear of getting hurt. We were then all in tears—when we give to others we nourish our hearts.

In giving, you receive. Again, it's the law of cause and effect. When you give something to someone else, you are often the one who feels best. Your basic goodness shines through. Have you ever given your time to help someone with a flat tire, given directions to someone who is lost, given up your seat to someone who needs it more, or simply given support to someone having a bad day? What happens to you inside? I'll bet those small acts of generosity are often the highlight of your day. Everyone is better off and you get a helper's high.

> In giving, you receive. Again, it's the law of cause and effect.
> •

As Ralph Waldo Emerson explains, "It is one of the beautiful compensations of this life that no man can sincerely help another without helping himself."

Recently I decided to wrap up and cash in a basket of coins I had accumulated. Every day when I get home I empty whatever change is in my pocket into this basket. In the past, the change would disappear as my children would pick through it for extra spending money. Now in an empty nest, it was overflowing. So I threw the change in a bag and took it to the local grocery store where there was an automatic coin sorter.

It was Christmas season, and as I was entering the store, an old friend of mine was ringing the bell at a Salvation Army donation stop. I spontaneously handed the bag of coins to him and we instantly broke into laughter and appreciation for what we were both doing. That moment stuck with me and was a source of joy and comfort for days.

Many of our world traditions point to the value of generosity to our happiness as well as our success. Today's research agrees that volunteer activity induces a sense of well-being, and that giving is an essential component of good mental health. The whole field of servant leadership has emerged from the notion that it is in our own self-interest to take into account the self-interest of others. Even Adam Smith would admit that. Servant leaders succeed because the needs of followers are so looked after that they reach their full potential and perform at their best.

Generosity takes many forms. You can give money, you can give time, you can give a piece of yourself. These are all important, but I think what is most important for our happiness is our attitude. Does your generosity feel like single acts of giving, as in donating to your favorite cause each year, or is it more of a way of life? I don't mean giving everything away, I mean giving in different ways and within your means wherever opportunities arise. Who is more generous, for instance, Bill Gates who makes a one-time gift of half of his fortune to create a foundation in his name, or the mother in Darfur who gives up meals each and every day so her children can eat? Both are important, of course; but I argue that the benefits to your happiness are greater if your giving is more of a way of life and you don't expect recognition in return.

There is an ancient Buddhist metaphor about this. It asks, *Do you give as a king* who magnanimously shares his wealth with his people after it is gained, or *do you give as a boatman* who ferries himself and others across the river safely together, or *do you give as a shepherd* who makes sure his flock is always in front and arrives safely first? Which do you think induces a greater sense of well-being?

I haven't always given of myself, but I have learned to *behave into a new way of being*. I remember debating with a friend, for instance, about how I wanted to be more generous in my feelings with others but couldn't. Since I didn't *feel* generous, I argued, how I could I be generous? Finally one day I just tried complimenting a friend, even though it didn't feel quite natural to me at the time. Surprisingly, not only was he was moved, but so was I! Offering the compliment allowed me to connect with him, and I felt better about myself. My acting generously aroused feelings of generosity.

Later, at a support team meeting, this issue of giving of myself came up again. People weren't satisfied with what they were getting from me. So they challenged me to go around the circle and take turns sitting in front of each one of them. They wanted me to look into each person's eyes, and then express what I saw and what I felt. To my amazement, pressed in this way, my intuition and my heart came rushing forth. Somehow, on a gut level, I knew both the gifts and the challenges each person had in this life and pointed to them accurately. In expressing this in words, I also felt my appreciation of them and compassion for them and was very moved. In those few moments, I gave myself totally over to each one of my friends and discovered a gift that I always thought was missing but was really there all along.

This way of giving is now an integral part of my life as a friend, as a mentor, and as a professional coach. I spend much of my days in this role, and over the years I am being transformed by it. My listening skills have improved, my compassion is deeper, and my emotions are more easily expressed. I also have a stronger sense of confidence and self-worth. In exercising my basic goodness, I develop basic goodness. I am completely comfortable now with others and spend little time worrying about me.

Winston Churchill said, "We make a living by what we get, we make a life by what we give."

Follow the signs

When you pay attention and open to the world, you can see its patterns, and these patterns can help guide you. They show up as little synchronicities, and these synchronicities give you messages—messages that can help you in the choices you make. Have you ever been faced with a decision and then receive a "sign" or omen for which way to go?

The old saying is that synchronicity is God's way of remaining anonymous. In explaining how it happens, Jung said your habitual thoughts—both conscious and unconscious—combined with your daily activities cause you to manifest them. Subconsciously you know what you want, and through that you attract events or messages which if you follow them will lead to important life lessons.

> The old saying is that synchronicity is God's way of remaining anonymous.

Several important synchronicities have happened in my life. The raccoon story is one that I already shared. Another is how I found my current professional role, the one that I feel is the answer to my calling.

I had grown stale in my old work and began thinking how to make a change, perhaps into full time consulting in leadership; but with two teenagers at home, this was a bit of a risky move. So one day at work I was on the way to the bathroom and I just randomly grabbed the university job listings on the way. Now, I never *ever* read these listings, but I did it this time just for entertainment. I opened it up, and there was the ad for the job I now have. My reaction was immediate: "That position has my name on it." It was only posted once and never again, and six weeks later I was in my new role.

A final story I want to share is about a workshop just months before the start of my midlife troubles you're by now quite familiar with. For this workshop we were asked to keep our real identities secret and to take an assumed name, one that had some personal significance. I took the name of the biblical character Job because I remembered him for his undying faith and found that inspiring. The thing that I *didn't* remember is that God challenged Job's faith to truly see whether Job's piety was really only as good as his prosperity. God ended up taking everything away: his family, his wealth, and even his health to test him. Yet Job held true.

Within a year of that workshop, I found myself in a similar situation, on the brink of losing everything—wife, house, children, job—as I struggled with my doubt. Taking the name of Job seemed like it had been a premonition of things to come. Yet as I reflected on it, I remembered why I took Job's name—his faith never wavered. And that thought helped again and again to inspire me to work my way through a difficult time.

Synchronicities happen every day, but we are often so consumed with our lives that we don't see them. To see them, you have to slow down, pay attention, and focus on your intentions. You will draw them to you. If you open outward and peel back the hindrances of self-concern that silence the heart, you will see them.

Exercise 36: Tracking synchronicity

    1. Pay careful attention when synchronicities occur in your life. Write them down and describe what happened. If you aren't sure

yet what synchronicity is, read *Jung on Synchronicity and the Paranormal* by Carl Jung or *Synchronicity: The Inner Path to Leadership* by Joe Jowarski. The latter is the story of a man who followed the signs in finding his calling.

2. Consider that they were not just meaningless coincidences and that they carry a message. What are they trying to tell you?

3. Try to make more happen by expecting certain things. Put your intention, or a question you have, into the world and then expect an answer. Look for signs and messages. You won't always receive them, but often you will.

7

Be Heroic

"You enter the forest at the darkest point, where there is no path. Where there is a way or path, it is someone else's path, you are not on your own path. If you follow someone else's way, then you are not going to realize your potential. It takes courage to do what you want, other people have lots of plans for you. Nobody wants you to do what you want to do, they want you to go on their trip."

—Joseph Campbell

IN *The Hero with a Thousand Faces,* Joseph Campbell showed us the universal myth of the Hero's Journey that traditional stories in all world cultures commonly express. In this myth, life circumstances force the hero to venture into the unknown, face tests and ordeals, undergo personal transformation, and then return to share with others the boons and lessons learned. Campbell saw this journey as a spontaneous production of the psyche and an archetypal process that portrays our search for meaning in a tale of separation, initiation, transformation, and return. He compared the stories of Osiris, Prometheus, Moses, Buddha, and Christ, for example, and showed how they follow the structure of this myth very closely.

Today's management literature also draws on this myth in showing how well-known contemporary leaders have been shaped by certain tests along their way. Warren Bennis calls them *crucibles* which he describes as a trial, a challenge, or a point of deep reflection that forces the question of who you are and what is important to you. Often crucibles inspire self-discovery, or a new altered sense of identity. They can be brought on by "big" life events such as illness, job loss, and travel, or by more mundane events such as a conversation with a mentor, a work challenge, or a personal problem. Our world is rich with stories of leaders whose lives were transformed by such crucibles, challenges, or moments of truth that shaped the values and attitudes that have made them successful. I shared a number of those stories in my book, *The Leadership Wheel*.

> It is a story in which people break away from conditioned and habitual patterns, enter into the unknown to rediscover lost parts of themselves, and return to share what they have learned . . .
>
> •

Fundamentally the Heroic Journey is about an inner quest to awaken the self to its fullest potential. It is a story in which people break away from conditioned projections, mental models, and habitual patterns; enter into the unknown to rediscover lost parts of their selves; learn to experience life more fully, openly, and directly; and return to share what they have learned in order to make the world better. Instead of serving self-interest, they serve self-discovery and the pursuit of wisdom. Having discovered it, they return to solve problems in the world.

Heroic people, however, are not always bigger than life. They are often normal people like you or me who struggle with life's challenges. This heroism is in anyone able to step out of their comfort zone, their cocoon, their box, and so on, to face risks and challenges of personal change despite fears, uncertainties, or circumstances. We have all faced fears that come with doing something new or different. For some, it may be launching a career, getting married, or traveling abroad. For others, it is trying to resolve a conflict that you have been avoiding, or taking a stand on an issue that you believe in. For still others, it may be a lack of inspiration, a recurring challenge, or the loss of a job.

Anytime you refuse to cope with a challenging life-situation you sell yourself short, restrict your consciousness, succumb to your doubts, and allow your deepest desires and needs to go unmet. Instead of rising to the opportunity the challenge presents, you hold on to what you have, defend your turf tightly, and barely get a breath of fresh air.

To travel your heroic path calls you to wake up and make a difference in your life. You can live the scripts, boxes, or expectations handed to you by others, or you can live by your own design through making conscious choices. This is not as far out of reach as you might think. Rather, it is often a process that begins right where you are, in the here and now of your everyday life. Any challenge, big or small, is an opportunity to break through the boxes of doubt and fear to achieve more than you believe possible. Just do this over and over again because as you do, you will discover that every fear or challenge you face is a vehicle for waking up.

So anytime you face one, you have a choice. You can slip into a malaise and lackluster effort, or heed the heroic call and choose a new way of life. There is nothing more ennobling of the human spirit than heeding this call. But doing that is not easy. It takes courage and commitment to go against the grain. To live a full life, you need to find the strength to find our own way.

Here are some tips how.

Reap the lessons of adversity

An early crucible for me was the sport of wrestling. I started wrestling as a young teenager and quickly found that it didn't come naturally. I often found myself on the losing end of my matches. I didn't want to quit because I grew up in a neighborhood where we all wrestled. It was the way we were to start making our mark on life, and I had a lot friends and family members I didn't want to disappoint or have think badly of me. Yet I felt I was failing.

I knew I had something, however, that many of the others didn't—discipline and the ability to work hard. So I just decided to work harder than everyone else. I practiced more, drilled more, and conditioned more. I drove my friends nuts, even wore them out with wanting to work so much. Soon enough I improved, stopped embarrassing myself, and eventually competed at a championship level.

From that experience I learned that no matter how tough the circumstances, if I were just disciplined and worked hard enough, eventually I would do fine. It was all in my control. It gave me a great sense of confidence and independence to know this, and I drew on that lesson again and again—first in schoolwork and then later in traveling, professional life, and so on.

> You can draw on the lessons of your own experience to help you face the tests of adversity.
> •

You can draw on the lessons of your own experience to help you face the tests of your journey. We all have times in life when we face difficulty and learn to deal with it in a way that pushes us to a higher level of growth and understanding. This could be coping with the loss of someone dear, adjusting to separation or divorce, overcoming an addiction or health problem, and so on. Rising to such challenges can reveal your true abilities and talents, your priorities, and your own real philosophy of life. The key is to make sense and derive meaning from these tough times. Through adversity you come into your own and fathom your mettle; and in so doing, you galvanize and shape a new sense of self.

I learned even more from wrestling. Later, in college I had the urge to become an Olympian. It was plausible, as my coach was the captain of the previous Olympic team and two of my wrestling partners were former national intercollegiate champions. They all encouraged me to set my goals high. I worked hard and they helped develop my skill to a much higher level. Yet still I wasn't happy.

I was winning, but not as much as I and everyone thought I should have been. My heart wasn't in it. I had been doing it for others all along and just fell into the habit of continuing. Eventually, I started to look closely at what it really took to compete in the Olympics. I realized that it simply demands too much and would make my life too narrow for my taste. So I quit after my sophomore year. My coach, my mother and my stepfather, and my college roommates put tremendous pressure on me to return, thinking that if I quit wrestling then I would quit school. But I knew from my previous lesson that I would be fine, and this sport was no longer for me.

As soon as I made that decision, my whole world seemed to open up. I started to read for leisure again to learn about things I was interested in, was able to get odd jobs and save money to travel, and was free to meet and make new and interesting friends. I even tried football, a sport for which I had a true love, and immediately excelled. It was the first time in my life that I learned to *follow my bliss*, and a lesson I would never forget.

We all have experiences we can draw on in forging our own path. They often point to the sources of our resilience. Where have you been heroic in facing a crucible in your life? What were the inner resources that you drew on? How were you changed? How can you apply them now?

Exercise 37: The Heroic Journey

Select a story in which you faced a crucible or were heroic in dealing with a challenge or adversity in your life—one that had a significant impact and through which you were personally inspired or changed.

1. What were the fears, insecurities, and demons you had to face?
2. What inner resources did you draw on in facing them?
3. What were the lessons learned and how did you change?
4. What happened to your attitude towards life and old relationships afterwards?

Turn fear into an ally

When I was a boy, I was so terrified of heights that I would panic simply by being around a ladder. This panic was beyond a healthy fear of heights—I would freeze. Then as a young man I had an opportunity to go rock climbing in a wilderness adventure program. I was determined to face my fear, so I was the first to go up. The climb was about eighty feet with an eighty percent pitch.

I had cotton-mouth, I was gripped, I slipped a couple times, but I muscled my way through it. Even though I was safely on the end of a rope, I was still terrified. Then the instructor said, "Now I want you to do it again blindfolded." Panic set in again; but not to be outdone by my peers, who I knew were going to do it, I did it one more time with the blindfold.

The result was amazing to me. I felt more in control without my sight. I was able to turn my vision inward and saw how my fear was just an idea about being out of control and was very workable.

My breakthrough was invigorating, and emboldened me to tackle other fears such as speaking up in a group and working through conflicts with others. It also proved to be extremely helpful in dealing with many other fears that arose in midlife. I drew on this experience again and again in facing my demons.

Emerson said, "Always do what you are afraid to do." Traveling your own path requires learning to work with fear. We all have fears, many of them rooted in self-doubt. But there are healthy fears like a fear of heights (mine went beyond healthy)—even avid rock climbers have this fear—and then there are unhealthy fears. The unhealthy fears are the ones that signal the way to our personal growth: *Our hang-ups contain our wealth and our neurosis our wisdom.*

> Emerson said, "Always do what you are afraid to do."

Unhealthy fear shapes the boundaries of what we know and feel possible. These fears are different for each of us. For some it may be a fear of public speaking: "I freeze in front of groups so I can't do that." For others it may be a feeling of being out of control: "I can't let them do that, they would do it wrong." For still others it is losing our job, going to parties, or saying something stupid. I even knew a person who was afraid of Claymation of all things! These unhealthy fears make us small.

Whatever that boundary is for you, cross it. I had a fear of heights, I crossed it. I had a fear of being exposed in groups, I crossed it. I had a fear of public speaking, I crossed it. I had a fear of being vulnerable in relationship, and I crossed it. There is much growth in crossing the threshold of your fears.

In my experience, crossing them requires three things: awareness, courage, and action.

It requires awareness because when you are aware you see the world more accurately, and this helps diffuse your emotional reactions. Your fear often comes from what you don't know. You may not order something new off the menu, for instance, for fear of not liking it; or you don't address a conflict for fear of a bad outcome. More poignantly, fear comes from not wanting to know what you don't know. You may not ask for feedback, for instance, for fear it might be bad; or you don't ask someone out on a date for fear of their lack of interest. When you are aware of these fears, however, and their habitual causes, their grip begins to loosen. Notice your fears as they arise and ask about their root. I'm aware, for instance, that I tend to avoid asking for a date because I'm afraid of rejection. So I ask myself, What are the consequences? I quickly see not much—just a wounded pride—so why not?

It also takes courage even to ask these questions, but we often confuse courage with fearlessness. Courage is not the absence of fear but transcending it by deciding that something else is more important. True courage is learning to work through your fear, and when you do, it feels like a breakthrough. Have you ever noticed, for instance, that when you work through your fear, it creates an uplifting, exhilarating energy? Like the feeling I had in working with my fear of heights. You have broken through a self-imposed limitation, and that instills a confidence you can ride for further change.

Finally it requires action. Have you ever felt nervous, for instance, before confronting a difficult conversation, or making a big presentation, and then seen your nervousness disappear soon after you start? It was that way with me in athletics—nervous as I entered into competition but relaxed soon after the action began. The best remedy for dealing with fear is to act. Action dissolves the fear.

> The best remedy for dealing with fear is to act.
> •

Exercise 38: Turn fears into breakthroughs

1. Make a list of fears that people commonly have. Make it as long as possible.
2. Which of these fears are ones that you have from time to time?
3. What do you do about it when you experience it? Do you move away, or move towards it?
4. What do you need to know to help move towards it and take

action? What questions do you need to ask? What support do you need?

5. Choose a fear that's common for you, and challenge yourself with it the next time it arises. Just step into it.

Push your edge

Taking *turn fear into an ally* one step further is to learn to *push your edge*. One of the most interesting insights I have learned to appreciate over the years is the amazing growth in learning, confidence, and happiness that happens when we step out of our comfort zones. We all know what a comfort zone is—everything inside our protective wall of accumulated habits, attitudes, beliefs, and mental models that develop over years of conditioning. These set up the emotional, cultural, and intellectual space inside which we feel safe. This comfort zone tells us what is expected and accepted and *its edge is often defined by our fear or our laziness.* Sometimes our comfort zone is helpful and useful, while at other times it makes us complacent, stuck, and small.

> This comfort zone tells us what is expected and accepted and its edge is often defined by our fear or our laziness.
> •

What holds you in situations that no longer work for you often is habit, procrastination, and fear. Until you can let go of the old, worn-out habits, they'll continue to hold you prisoner. You may not like your relationship, or you may feel you are overweight, yet you are comfortable and won't move because of laziness or fear of uncertainty. This only condemns you to frustration and regret. But as Campbell said, "We must be willing to let go of the life we have planned, so as to accept the life that is waiting for us."

When you push the edge of your comfort zone, you learn and grow. Your world expands. A friend once told me "If you want something you've never had, then you must do something you have never done." If you don't like the job you are in and long for something else, then you are going to have to risk the change.

Lots of people who suffer from boredom at work are *doing it to them-*

selves. They're bored and frustrated because that's what their choices have caused them to be. They're stuck in ruts they've dug for themselves while trying to avoid making mistakes and taking risks. People who never make mistakes, never make anything else either.

A former student of mine was a financial manager and miserable from the drudgery of his work. So he quit to pursue his first love of writing and is now a successful playwright. Many of us know of people like this who were willing to take the risk and try something new. Almost every job I ever took I was not qualified for in the beginning. It was always a stretch, and without taking that stretch I never would have found the work that I love to do.

Once you have some success with this approach, you gain confidence to try even more new things. I remember my fear of learning to ride a bike as a child. I didn't want to fall and skin my knees or get hurt. But as learned to ride my confidence grew. I started turning corners, then learned to turn them faster, then began doing "wheelies," jumping over ramps, and so on. We have all experienced something similar. It's the same in learning a new language: If you're anything like me, you're probably afraid to try speaking out for fear of feeling embarrassed or stupid. The need to protect your "impeccable" self-image steps in to block the way. But when you give it an honest try, others begin to help, and soon you gain confidence.

Imagine if you spent a lifetime stepping out and stretching yourself like this? When I observe people my age, I see immediately who has learned to do this and who has not—the difference in confidence, success, even demeanor, is remarkable. People who haven't been heroic when they could, look older than they should, fail to look you in the eye, and hunch their shoulders as if they carry a lot of shame or regret. It's amazing.

Perhaps most importantly, pushing the edge of your comfort zone can make you happier. *Pushing your edge* wakes you up. You aren't operating from your typical frame of reference, so you become accessible and responsive, and experience your world more directly and freshly. You connect to your experience more intimately without rising above it. It's like breaking the shell of your protective egg and revealing the raw, more authentic you.

You are exposed and feel a soft spot that's vulnerable and tender—your basic goodness. Yes, it can be scary, embarrassing, and painful; but it doesn't mean throwing caution to the wind, it means learning to deal with the discomfort. It's one of the most important steps you can take in waking up your heart and mind. It is heroic.

Have you ever noticed how alive and present you feel when you take a risk? The colors are brighter, the mind is sharper, the body is aroused, and the heart is open. A great example of this that I often see is when people challenge themselves in workshops I lead. They take risks in sharing things they haven't shared before, doing role-plays and skits in front of strangers, and giving and receiving emotionally charged feedback. They struggle, they are tense, but they are very "on." They are also more open, vulnerable, and worthy. They immediately connect with others in the group on a deeper level by feeling compassion and pride for others doing the same thing. It is so powerful, it can be addictive.

So *pushing your edge* means acting courageously to challenge your stagnation and reactivity. It may also mean inviting a certain level of chaos and confusion, because it is only in learning to live in that space—beyond your comfort zone—that you truly relate directly and authentically to your world. It's about stepping into the uncertainty and fear, relating to your discomfort, and staying in touch with the heart-throbbing quality of being alive.

One of the best ways I know of working your edge is through travel. Traveling or working overseas literally distances you from your family, friends, culture, and even language. A different country means that you have no choice but to take chances.

My time in Nepal was my first exposure to the underdeveloped world and real poverty. The first day in Kathmandu I took a walk through the city, and was so taken by the lack of sanitation, health, cleanliness, and adequate clothing that I went back to the hotel disturbed. This was not going to be easy.

Soon I moved to a village and lived with a family. It was a family of twelve, living in a four-room mud hut with no running water, electricity, or even furniture; but since I was the honored guest, they gave me a whole room to myself. The very first night I was there, they asked if I was cold because I was hunched over sitting on the floor. I said yes, a little, so they started a fire of straw in front of me and the whole house filled with smoke.

They lived hand to mouth, were faced with the constant threat of disease, and suffered from so many disadvantages, but the last word I would use to describe them is unhappy. They smiled quickly and often, would do anything to help me, and were basically happy because their life was focused on family and community, and not acquisition. I learned so much about what was really necessary to be happy.

You never know what you are going to learn.

Another story I like from an unknown source is about a father in a very wealthy family who took his son on a trip to the country, with the express purpose of showing him how poor people live. They spent a couple days and nights on the farm of what would be considered a very poor family.

On their return from their trip, the father asked his son, "How was the trip?"

"It was great, Dad."

"Did you see how poor people live?" the father asked.

"Oh yeah," said the son.

"So, tell me, what did you learn from the trip?" asked the father.

The son answered, "I saw that we have one dog and they have four. We have a pool that reaches to the middle of our garden and they have a creek that has no end. We have imported lanterns in our garden and they have the stars at night. Our patio reaches to the front yard and they have the whole horizon. We have a small piece of land to live on and they have fields that go beyond our sight. We have servants who serve us, but they serve others. We buy our food, but they grow theirs. We have walls around our property to protect us, they have friends to protect them."

The father was speechless.

Then his son added, "Thanks, Dad, for showing me how poor we are."

But *pushing your edge* need not be something dramatic. What is most important is to learn to look at your life freshly without any veils and try new things. Start with simple things. Drive a different route home. Shop at a different grocery store. Try a new food. Make a conscious effort to experiment. This helps you develop new muscles of awareness, creativity, and perspective for seeing the world freshly.

Then kick it up a notch: Sign up for Toastmasters to push yourself in public speaking, or take the dance lessons that your partner wants you to, or start that writing course you've always wanted to try. You will feel awkward at first, but let yourself feel the tension and adrenaline rise a bit. Allow your anxiety level to increase. Feel your heart rate and breathing go faster. Adrenaline is your body's natural drug that, in moderation, makes you sharp, creative, and quick. It creates the feeling of excitement and exhilaration that comes from trying something new. Recognize that it also can be scary and stressful. Some stress is useful. Too much can be harmful. Find the right balance for you.

A final story I want to share on this topic is about when a friend talked me into attending a local psychodrama session. Psychodrama is a group technique that explores through role play the problems, issues, concerns, dreams, and so on of people and groups. In essence, each person in the group becomes a therapeutic agent for each other person in the group. As we began the session, the facilitator guided us through a check-in process and then asked everyone who they all wanted to work with that morning.

Since I was new, I was chosen. The facilitator then asked me what I wanted to work on. Without any premeditation at all, I just blurted out the day my father died. I had no idea where that thought came from.

For the next two hours, we re-enacted that day for me . . . switching into and out of various roles as we went along. I played me, my father, my grandmother, and so on as others did the same. I immediately burst into tears and sobbed through most of the session. I had no idea that I was still harboring such deep pain and resentment. In reflecting on it afterwards, the session proved incredibly important to helping me understand and dissolve some of my issues related to that event. I went back for another session later, but it wasn't the same. I never returned after that—I got what I needed in the first one.

Exercise 40: Stretch yourself

1. Make a list of fifty things that, if you were successful doing them, would make you more effective or more successful: give a speech, write and publish an article, start an exercise program, meditate daily, teach a class, feed a homeless person, volunteer, climb a mountain, learn to play a new musical instrument, sign up for a dance class, try for that new client, and so on.

2. From your list, choose one or two that you're willing to do within the next ninety days. Schedule those one or two new activities, then go for it. Afterward, choose one or two more and do it again. Make exercising these new muscles a lifelong habit.

Don't try to escape

One of my favorite books is *The Wisdom of No Escape,* by Pema Chodron. The title captivates me because it conveys so much wisdom so simply. The central message is to try not to run away from the suffering our life issues cause. She says, "You can leave your marriage, you can quit your job, you can go where people are going to praise you, you can manipulate your world until you are blue in the face, but the same old demons will always come until you finally have learned your lesson. The lesson they came to teach you."

Our painful emotions are like beacons showing the way to our freedom...telling us to wake up and lean into a situation when we would rather cave in and back away.
•

Our painful emotions are like beacons showing the way to our freedom, or red flags saying "You're stuck!" They are telling us to wake up and lean into a situation when we would rather cave in and back away.

When we are aware of these emotions, we have an opportunity of staying with them instead of spinning out. Spinning out is letting one negative thought lead to another in a way that builds an energy and momentum all of its own. When I was young and dating, for instance, I would often find myself worrying, "What if she doesn't call? Is she with someone else? I'll give her another hour then I'll be sure. I bet I know who it is." Sound familiar? Or is it just my abandonment issue again?

Then she would call and I would be fine. I had gotten all worked up, yet nothing had happened. It was all in my mind.

With awareness, however, you can gently catch yourself in the moment before you are swept away and your thoughts and feelings solidify. It's about nipping it in the bud. "There it is again. You know what this is about. Take a deep breath and let it go." Bring your awareness to your issue as it arises, and eventually it will dissolve. Simply stay with the uncertainty and anxiety, and it will begin to break up. This is easier said than done. Loosening the habitual pattern of the negative emotion often requires coming back to it over and over again.

Pulling the plug on these patterns requires practice, so sometimes it's helpful to bring your issues to you, invite them in, and face them down. I know this might sound a little crazy, but try consciously bringing your issue to mind: Imagine the worst, look at it, let it go; then relax, and do the whole process over and over again.

If I fear, for instance, that someone I want to see is going to be with someone else, I bring it to mind, imagine it happening, and immerse myself in the fear. I stick with the fear, and eventually it begins to break up and I relax. Once you visualize like this, the outcome just happens naturally. In doing this a number of times deliberately, as a practice, you will be ready to catch the emotion when it arises for real.

Another trick I use is to visualize that my basic goodness is the bright shining sun and my negative emotions are the clouds moving past and obscuring it. When I have problems that bring up emotions that make me want to cave, I just rest my attention on the sun and its rays burn those clouds away. Again, you do this over and over.

What life issue might you want to work with in one of these ways?

Your *real* life issues will haunt you until you deal with them. They can be rooted in any number of things—a fear of being out of control, not feeling recognized, feeling abandoned, and so on—and they often show up most poignantly in romantic relationships. Have you ever noticed how some people are attracted to the same type of person in one unsuccessful relationship after another—to someone who is distant, or who is smothering, or who is domineering, or . . .? As we discussed before, there are many reasons for this—but the question is: How do you deal with it? Unfortunately, today's world makes it easy to switch partners when a relationship isn't working, but then the pattern just tends to repeat itself.

My abandonment issue, for instance, led me into a pattern of failed relationships. I smothered my high school and college girlfriends in seeking the kind of attention I wanted. It was a turn-off for them, of course. In my mid-twenties I was with a person who actually was as attentive as I thought I wanted; but that, oddly enough, was a turn-off for me. It seemed the chemistry of my attraction only worked for more distant women.

Then there was the relationship with my wife. At first I met her pulling away with a modicum of reason and balance. Gradually I began to feel this was becoming an "unfair" loss. Before too long I was even feeling like Job, feeling a sense of loss that evoked my deepest fears. In trying to hold on, I lost my sense of self. I gave myself away, imitated what others wanted, and started to make poor decisions.

If I had known then how to enter into those fears as I've since learned to do, things may have worked out differently. No doubt I would have acted differently.

Instead, after the divorce, things got even worse. I entered the most difficult relationship of my life. It was like the Universe would not turn me loose, like something was committed to making me see the pattern I had to change in order to grow. She was a strong, distant woman, and soon my issue was raging again; but this time something shifted in me. I realized she was not emotionally available to explore a deeper understanding of our issues; so rather than hang on in self-doubt as I had done so often before, I ended the relationship.

It was only at this point that I first began to really work with my life pattern. Who was I attracted to and why? What were the underlying causes? When things didn't work out, why did I hold on so much? This last one clearly was the key question: Why did I cling to it in the way I did? I realized that I couldn't help who I'm attracted to psycho-emotionally, but I could learn to deal with how I relate to the emotions it brings up in the moment.

I fell in love two more times over the next few years, but was very conscious to not cling. I learned to *embrace the beloved.* These were healthy relationships that eventually ended because of changing life circumstances. Still, each time, as we began to separate, my fear arose again; but I worked with it differently. Instead of clinging and holding on, I learned to stay open, remain vulnerable, pay attention to what I was feeling, let go, and flow into the hurt and pain over and over again. I consciously brought my fears to mind, and then let them go. We also dialogued to gain a deeper understanding and appreciation of one another and our circumstances. We separated with dignity and without any negative residue, and remain good friends to this day.

Something very profound happened to me in this process. In looking back, I saw my pattern and its source very clearly. I also noticed that after every break-up, I managed not only to survive but to recover and remain open-hearted. I discovered my resilience, my basic goodness, in an even deeper way. I realized in a deep way that my self-worth does not depend on a woman I'm with, or the father I never had, but on me. Sure, I knew this intellectually early on, but I had to experience it in my heart before I could go free of the pattern. As the romantic phase of each of the last two relationships mentioned here ended, I was both sad and happy at the same time. How odd—but it was my truth.

As this huge life issue for me began to dissolve, the positive feelings that emerged emboldened me in other areas of my life. If I can recover from painful relationships every time, I thought, why not enter the next with courage and whole-heartedness? In fact, why not enter every relationship that way—whether it's with lovers, family, friends, or colleagues? It doesn't matter if I get hurt—I'll be fine, I'll still happy, and maybe even a little more resilient. I began to step into every aspect of my life—work, friendships, relationships—with more self-awareness, connectedness, emotional freedom, expressiveness, vulnerability, sense of service, and authenticity. I learned to "be at cause" (meaning, serving my mission) in every activity I engaged in or relationship I had. I like to believe it has made me a better friend, colleague, coach, facilitator, lover, maybe even writer!

In the end, I guess I learned to love more deeply through seeing there's a difference between love and being in love. Being "in love" is often a precursor to love . . . but it's based on projecting our own needs outward, and that projecting is based on our wounds. That's not love—it's a state of co-dependence that has its roots in a sense of unworthiness. Only in discovering your basic goodness can you dislodge that sense of unworthiness and stop the projections. That's when true love can begin. My abandonment issue had held me back and obscured my basic goodness, but not anymore.

As I gained this growing sense of freedom from my self-doubt, I felt I was moving from a sense of

Poverty	to	Abundance
Dependence	to	Interdependence
Control	to	Surrender
Narrowness	to	Expansiveness
Doubt	to	Confidence
Projection	to	Nakedness
For me	to	For them
Ambivalence	to	Integrity
Other-affirmed	to	Self-affirmed

For several years now, I've been happier, more successful, and more productive than ever before in my life. The freedom I yearned for in my opening journal entry seems to be coming to fruition.

Don't get me wrong, I only claim to have learned a few things worth knowing—I'm far from free of falling victim to my issues from time to time. I'm just not their constant prisoner, and when I do get into trouble with them, I can find my way out pretty quickly. It's much easier to let go of them when you're confident that the basic goodness inside you will see you through if you stay open to it.

> If you constantly challenge your life issue, whatever it is, you gradually dissolve it over time: In going into the fire, you eventually see you will not wither.
>
> •

This was my path and my issue, but everyone's journey is different. If you constantly challenge your life issue, whatever it is, you gradually dissolve it over time: In going into the fire, you eventually see you will not wither. You discover your basic goodness.

I have a friend, for instance, whose life issue is about being taken advantage of. As the oldest in her family for four children, she was constantly asked to care for her younger siblings, take the lead in doing the chores, and so on. She learned to be accepted by just giving in to the demands. As an adult, this way of operating caused her great heartache as she often felt dismissed at work and at home. Gradually she learned to stand up to her parents, her boss, her colleagues, her husband, and even her own children. As she did, she found doing so less and less scary and realized that her world would not cave in if she just said no. In the process, just as in my case, she eventually discovered her worth and her world gradually turned around.

As I said before, most of our life issues revolve around and can only be resolved through relationships. You can do therapy, you can read books, and you can go to workshops—all of which can help—but you will only be successful by working through the issue as it manifests in your relationships. So *don't try to escape* as it rears its ugly head. Instead, with courage, commitment, and vulnerability *embrace the beloved* as well as any of the other healthy mental models here that work for you.

The most interesting thing for me is that as my psychological issues resolved, my metaphysical interests heightened. As I said in the introduction, for me there seem to be three phases to life. The hungry spirit never seems to let go: As one crisis gets resolved, it moves on to other greater things. Life brings more, not less to deal with. You may find this to be true for you, too.

The truth is, *we are all sleeping gods.* But as a friend once said to me, to learn to surrender to the divine you must first understand who and what you are, because you can only surrender from a place of worth, not from a place of fear.

Whatever that next step means to you, my only hope is to be helpful as a ferryman.

8
Enjoy the Ride

"Imagination was given to man to compensate him for what he is not; a sense of humor to console him for what he is."

—Sir Francis Bacon

S O, WE HAVE SEEN there is this longing, hungry spirit that you can ride, if you choose, to your freedom and a greater sense of who you are.

That ride can make you not only happier but also a more effective human being. To stay on and not fall off, you have to balance your self-interest with a caring for the well-being of whole. This balance is the key to discovering your basic goodness and your highest, most authentic self.

The real challenge of the journey, of course, is to change you and the world from right where you are, one step at a time. It is about learning to leave your scripted ways behind to find the real you. It is about learning how to tap into and then bring your natural gifts and passions forth into the world, and make a positive contribution with them. It is also about learning how to empower others to do the same.

But lest we take ourselves too seriously on this journey, there is another healthy mental model to share, and that is to *enjoy the ride*.

I hope the benefits of humor are clearly evident to you. Socially, it's been said that humor is the shortest distance between two people—it relieves tension, invites openness, and puts things in perspective. It also lowers blood pressure, boosts the immune system, and improves brain functioning. In the workplace, it improves morale, reduces stress, increases productivity, and enhances the development teams. As Milton Berle liked to say, "Laughter is an instant vacation!"

So why don't we see more of it?

Research shows that by the time children reach nursery school they laugh an average of three hundred times per day, but adults laugh only seventeen times per day. It's another one of those conditioned habits—as we grow older, we place more importance on our activities and perhaps begin to take ourselves too seriously. Much of this is due to taking on more responsibility; but in the end, there is really no conflict between taking our responsibilities seriously and ourselves lightly.

We all have tendencies to blow events out of proportion, demand perfection, and behave as if our needs are the center of everything. People are never so trivial as when they take themselves so seriously. I know an attorney who insists on having her assistant sharpen her pencils instead of doing it herself, a social activist who sharply criticized another for not knowing "undocumented" is a more politically correct term than "illegal" immigrant, and an academic who insists on being addressed Dr. simply because he has a Ph.D. My favorite, though, is a Buddhist who beats himself up for not feeling compassion for his dog that just taken a crap on the floor. Lighten up!

If you aren't careful, you can get so hung up on yourself that you lose your grip on reality and begin to get tight. You want the world to conform to your way, and when it doesn't you try to force it and everything gets distorted. You wrestle over the wording of each e-mail, lay awake each night anticipating the events of the next day, and scrutinize the minutest detail of an event. "Was I good enough?" "Will I get it right?"

Humor shifts this way of thinking. Remember, it's not the situation that causes you stress, it's the meaning you place on the situation. Humor adjusts the meaning of a situation so it's not so overwhelming. It diffuses the tension and opens you to new perspectives and mental models. Your actions may not be as important as you naturally suppose. Laughing at yourself and the situation helps reveal that small things are not as earthshaking as they sometimes seem to be. It is also disarming to others and makes you more real.

Self-effacing humor really helps you take your attention off yourself. I often make fun about my inattention to detail or for being such an intro-vert. I don't use them as an excuse for my shortcomings, but I do like to tell stories about them. This makes me more approachable, especially in working with students. Otherwise they tend to relate to me with so much "respect" that it becomes a barrier. I share this with my children and they say, "Jeez, Dad, if they only knew who you *REALLY* are!"

Enjoy the ride is not about cracking jokes or making fun at someone else's expense, it's about taking a basic cheerful and playful attitude towards life. You don't need to become a comedian, but you can learn to play with your reality and pop the distorted sense of importance that you give it. I can make fun of myself for wearing the same pants two days in a row, or make a witty response to someone's comments, especially when they seem filled with self-importance.

I was caught not too long ago bragging about a squash game I had just won, so my assistant deadpans, "I am so happy for you." We all broke up in laughter. We all can play with life like this. I have always been teased, not in a demeaning way, but in an endearing way. Why? Because I play while I work and invite others to do the same.

As I said before, playfulness does not mean ignoring your responsibili-ties or not taking them seriously. It's about finding and taking joy in your work and your responsibilities. Like many others, I'm a playful dad, and that is not an oxymoron. I believe being playful makes me a better dad. Similarly, in terms of seeking happiness, it is about having fun in pursu-ing the hard work that we have set out to do. *It is not work hard and play hard—it is play while you work.*

This takes no special talent, skill, or training, and it doesn't require a Masters degree or a license. It's about standing back from your situation, and learning to put things in perspective by finding the humor in it. It's not about ignoring responsibilities, it's about being light-hearted about your reality. Play and laugh—it loosens your tight grip on yourself and broadens your perspective. Doing this renews your energy, connects you to others, and helps you work with sticky issues.

Do things that make you laugh. Be silly at times, play with your own and others' habits and tendencies, tell a joke (if you can remember them, I can't), or share a funny story from your life (my favorite).

Young children are often a great source for funny stories. One of my favorites is from the day my son was born. I went to dinner with another father whose son was also born that day, and we had our two three-year-old children with us. We went to a Chinese restaurant and sat in a booth with the two children facing the two fathers. After a few minutes, his son leaned over to my daughter and asked if she had a penis. My daughter, already well-schooled by her mother, said, "No, I have a vulva." The boy's eyes grew huge, and says, "Wow, a Volvo, how did you get that!?"

Remember, have fun along the way.

Identifying Your Strengths: The Leadership Wheel Assessment

THIS SERIES OF QUESTIONS is designed to help assess your current talents with regard to each of the directions of the Wheel. Although this assessment is designed as a self-assessment, it also can be given to others for their perspective. Having others also complete the assessment—indicating what they see as true for you—can provide powerful additional feedback and insight.

Using a total of ten points for *each* of the paired five-item sets below, divide the points in any way you wish among the five choices. Assign more points to the characteristics you feel are more like you or the individual being scored, and less, or even zero, to the others. Be sure to use ten points for each of the five-item sets, assigning an overall total of fifty points through the five sets.

Set 1

1 ___ would rather generate and build on ideas than implement them   ___ is perceived as creative and an explorer of ideas

2 ___ chooses to be more thoughtful than spontaneous   ___ is seen as an objective and clear thinker

3 ___ prefers to implement ideas rather than discuss them   ___ is able to get things done

4 ___ tends to value feeling and process more than ideas   ___ major focus is relationship and interaction with people

5 ___ is open and flexible to new directions   ___ is patient and allows events to unfold

Set 2

6	___ is seen as a divergent thinker who seeks new connections	___ is able to quickly prioritize and see what is most important	
7	___ is analytical and attentive to detail	___ is seen as rational and logical	
8	___ is recognized as result and action oriented	___ is decisive in moving things along	
9	___ is inclusive and seeks the input of others	___ is known as a natural networker, collaborator, and team player	
10	___ is considered agile and able to adapt to changing circumstances	___ is self-aware and knows strengths and weaknesses	

Set 3

11	___ is a natural caretaker and nurturer of people	___ is known for loyalty and dedication to people
12	___ is a far-sighted visionary and big-picture person	___ is future-oriented in addressing issues
13	___ is well-organized and methodical	___ is a critical evaluator of people and ideas
14	___ naturally takes charge of a situation	___ is known for being tenacious and persevering
15	___ has composure in stressful situations	___ is focused on learning and personal development

Set 4

16	___ naturally seeks information and data	___ is pragmatic when dealing with others
17	___ is emotionally resilient and naturally trusting of others	___ is driven by personal values and impact on people on the issues
18	___ sees clearly despite complexity	___ is recognized as quite intuitive and insightful
19	___ likes to get on with the task at hand	___ is seen as one who stands by their beliefs and walks the talk
20	___ is seen as comfortable in different situations	___ is known as calm and even-tempered

Set 5

21	___ is realistic in solving problems and addressing issues	___ is seen as knowledgeable and competent	
22	___ is competitive and seeks challenges	___ is seen as courageous and willing to take risks	
23	___ spends time supporting and helping others	___ is seen as warm and friendly	
24	___ is optimistic and able to make the most out of situations	___ is personally open and candid with others	
25	___ is a strategic and systems thinker	___ is inspirational and passionate about ideas and possibilities	

Step 2: Referring to the answers above, add together the two scores next to each question with the same number (questions 1 through 25) and place the total next to the corresponding number below. Then add the numbers down each column and place the total score in the spaces provided.

	Teacher	Nurturer	Visionary	Warrior	Sage
	2. _____	4. _____	1. _____	3. _____	5. _____
	7. _____	9. _____	6. _____	8. _____	10. _____
	13. _____	11. _____	12. _____	14. _____	15. _____
	16. _____	17. _____	18. _____	19. _____	20. _____
	21. _____	23. _____	25. _____	22. _____	24. _____
Totals	_____	_____	_____	_____	_____

Score Range

0–10   Very little access to this set of talents

11–20   Can use these talents if need to

21–30   Natural preference for these talents

30+   A very strong preference for these talents, but may overuse them or be too dependent on them

Step 3: Refer to your responses and the descriptions of each of the intelligences below with the following questions in mind:

1. What are your natural strengths and preferences? List the top five qualities.
2. How do these show up when you are at your best? Are there any others that you would add to your list? What do your parents, friends, colleagues, or your spouse say?
3. What are your weaknesses or areas that you might need to compensate for to create more balance? List the top five qualities.
4. Given this, what strategies would you use to play to your strengths and work around your weaknesses?

After doing the self-assessment, ask another person who knows you well to also do one for you as they see you. This helps to deepen awareness, self-understanding, and the impact you have on others.

Leadership Wheel Summary

A way of thinking about the five intelligences of The Leadership Wheel is that they are the different aspects of the hungry spirit that work together in a five-step cycle of learning and development, with each aspect having both wisdom and shadow qualities. The wisdom qualities are part of the greater spirit, and the shadow qualities part of the lesser. You access wisdom through openness, and descend into the shadow through holding on and shutting down. The wisdom quality becomes neurotic when you use it to validate yourself and serve self-interest. This is usually the result of a fear or insecurity that we have talked about and manifests as "hanging-on" to or "overplaying" an intelligence to the point of turning an inherent strength into a weakness. Teachers, for instance who hold too tightly to the powers of their intellect can become overly attached to their view and try to make everything black and white, yes or no, and stubbornly fixate on their ideas. The following is a summary of the talents, wisdoms, and shadows of the five intelligences.

Teacher: Intellectual intelligence—"analyzing." The talent of the Teacher rests on expertise and intellectual grasp of the profession and industry. Teachers' technical skill, rational thought, and objective minds enable them to see reality clearly and objectively.

Wisdom	Shadow
Intellectual curiosity	Fixated and tight
Logic and rationality	Rigid and inflexible
Objective and realistic	Need to be right
Methodical, orderly problem solver	Analysis paralysis
Focus on the present, specific, and concrete—facts, data, details	Inability to see the big picture
Technical knowledge and skills	Bogged down in detail
	Appears insensitive

Nurturer: Emotional intelligence—"connecting." Nurturers are able to recognize and manage the feelings and emotions of self and others. This makes them good at relationships. They care about people and working collaboratively toward common ends. They are socially skilled, good listeners, communicators, networkers, and team players.

Wisdom	Shadow
Emotionally aware and empathic	Overly sensitive
Focus on building relationships	Takes things personally
Collaborative and inclusive	Dependence
Values driven	Conflict averse, unassertive
Supportive and service oriented	Feels guilty about differences
Good listener and communicator	Pride

Visionary: Intuitive Intelligence—"planning." Visionaries are able to see the big picture and think strategically and systematically in a way that helps them see the opportunities and the possibilities. They also have a clear purpose and vision for what they are doing and the purpose that guides their actions. That vision serves to uplift aspirations, foster commitment, and galvanize others.

Wisdom	Shadow
Creative and innovative	Unfocused
Connects the dots and sees the big picture	Over-committed
Strategic, conceptual and abstract thinker	Impulsive
Passionate	Lacking follow-through
Able to see what is most important	Inattention to detail
Focuses on ideas, future, possibilities	Easily bored
Spontaneous	Dreamer and impractical

Warrior: Action Intelligence—"enacting." Warriors are task and result oriented, and able to get things done. They actualize plans, take control of a situation, challenge the process, and take risks and experiment to make things happen. More importantly, they walk the talk, model the way, and align their actions with their words and deeds.

Wisdom	Shadow
Task and results oriented	Busyness
Courageous and willing to take risks	Overly competitive and aggressive
Drive and ambition	Insensitivity
Authentic	Controlling
Strength and perseverance	Micro-managing
Discipline	Bulldozing
	Ready, fire, aim

Sage: Spiritual Intelligence—"reflecting." Effective leaders know themselves and what they have to offer. They are learners, know themselves, and are open, candid and humble in their striving to grow and develop. They feel empowered to make a difference and make the most out of any experience. This makes them agile and able to adapt to changing situations.

Wisdom	Shadow
Self-aware and reflective	Procrastination
Agility and balance	Inability to adapt
Balance	Complacency
Open and candid	Victim mentality
Calm and composed	Dullness
Optimism	Denial

Bibliography
(RELATED READING AND SOURCES)

Arbinger Institute. *Leadership and Self-Deception.* San Francisco: Berrett-Koehler, 2002.

Ben-Shahar, Tal. *Happier.* New York: McGraw Hill, 2007.

Bennis, Warren G. *On Becoming a Leader.* Reading, MA: Addison Wesley, 1989.

Bennis, Warren G., and Robert J. Thomas. *Geeks and Geezers.* Boston: Harvard Business School Press, 2002.

Block, Peter. *Stewardship: Choosing Self-Interest over Service.* San Francisco: Berrett-Koehler, 1993.

Bohm, David. *Unfolding of Meaning.* Loveland, CO: Foundation House, 1985.

Boyatzis, Richard, and Annie McKee. *Resonant Leadership.* Boston: Harvard Business School Press, 2005.

Buber, Martin. *I and Thou.* New York: Free Press, 1971.

———. *The Knowledge of Man.* Atlantic Highlands, NJ: Humanities Press, 1988.

Campbell, Joseph. *The Hero with a Thousand Faces.* Princeton, NJ: Princeton University Press, 1973.

Chodron, Pema. *The Wisdom of No Escape.* Cambridge, MA, Shambhala, 2001.

Collins, James. *Good to Great.* New York: Harper Business, 2001.

Csikszentmihalyi, Mihaly. *Flow.* New York: Harper Perennial, 1991.

Dalai Lama. *The Art of Happiness.* New York: Riverhead Books, 1998.

Ellinor, Linda, and Glenn Gerard. *Dialogue: Rediscover the Transforming Power of Conversation.* New York: John Wiley and Sons, 1998.

Frankl, Viktor E. *Man's Search for Meaning.* Boston: Beacon, 1984.

Fromm, Erich. *The Sane Society.* Greenwich, OH: Fawcett, 1955.

Gilbert, Daniel. *Stumbling on Happiness.* New York: Alfred A. Knopf, 2006.

Goldberg, Natalie. *Writing Down the Bones.* Boston: Shambhala, 1986.

Goldstein, Joseph. *Insight Meditation: The Practice of Freedom.* Boston: Shambhala, 1993.

Goleman, Daniel. *Destructive Emotions: How Can We Overcome Them?* New York: Bantam, 2003.

———. *Emotional Intelligence.* New York: Bantam, 1997.

———. *Working with Emotional Intelligence.* New York: Bantam, 2000.

Goleman, Daniel, Richard Boyatzis, and Annie McKee. *Primal Leadership.* Boston: Harvard Business School Press, 2002.

Greenleaf, Robert. "The Servant Leader." Robert K. Greenleaf Center, 1991.

Handy, Charles. *The Hungry Spirit: Beyond Capitalism.* New York: Broadway Books, 1998.

Hendrix, Harville. *Getting the Love You Want.* New York: Holt Paperbacks, 2001.

Jung, Carl G. *The Essential Jung.* Edited by A. Storr. Princeton, NJ: Princeton University Press, 1983.

———. ed. *Man and His Symbols.* New York: Doubleday, 1964.

———. *The Portable Jung.* New York: Viking Press, 1976.

Jaworski, Joseph. *Synchronicity: The Inner Path of Leadership.* San Francisco: Berrett-Koehler. 1996.

Koestenbaum, Peter. *Leadership: The Inner Side of Greatness*. San Francisco: Jossey-Bass, 1991.

Kolb, David. *Experiential Learning*. Englewood Cliffs, NJ: Prentice Hall, 1984.

Kornfield, Jack. *Meditation for Beginners*. Boulder, CO: Sounds True, 2008

Lyubomirsky, Sonja. *The How of Happiness*. New York: Penguin Press, 2007.

Maslow, Abraham. *Motivation and Personality*. New York: Harper, 1954.

Patterson, Kerry, Joseph Grenny, Ron McMillan, and Al Switzler. *Crucial Conversations*. New York: McGraw Hill, 2002.

Rao, Srikumar. *Are You Ready to Succeed?* New York: Hyperion, 2006.

Ray, Michael. *The Highest Goal*. San Francisco: Berrett-Koehler, 2004.

Ricard, Matthieu. *Happiness: A Guide to Developing Life's Most Important Skill*. New York: Little, Brown and Company, 2003.

Shantideva, *A Guide to the Bodhisattva Way of Life*, Vesna A. and Alan B. Wallace, trans. Ithaca, NY: Snow Lion Publications, 1997.

Shimhoff, Marci. *Happy for No Reason*. New York: Free Press, 2008.

Seligman, Martin. *Authentic Happiness*. New York: Free Press, 2002.

Trungpa, Chogyam. *Cutting through Spiritual Materialism*. Boston: Shambhala, 1987.

———. *The Great Eastern Sun*. Boston: Shambhala, 1999.

———. *Orderly Chaos: The Mandala Principle*. Boston: Shambhala, 1991.

———. *Shambhala: The Sacred Path of the Warrior*. Boston: Shambhala, 1988.

———. *Transcending Madness: The Experience of the Six Bardos*. Boston: Shambhala, 1992.

Wilson, Eric. *Against Happiness*. New York: Sarah Crichton Books, 2008.

Index

About the Author

C. CLINTON SIDLE is director of the prestigious Roy H. Park Leadership Fellows Program in the Johnson School of Graduate Management at Cornell University and a top consultant in strategic change, leadership, executive coaching, and developing human potential. He has worked with Fortune 500 companies, state and local educational systems, and some of the nation's leading universities and non-profit organizations. His leadership programs at Cornell and elsewhere have earned national recognition. Clint is also the author of two earlier books *High Impact Tools and Techniques for Strategic Planning* by McGraw Hill (1998) in collaboration with Rod Napier and Pat Sanaghan, and *The Leadership Wheel: Five Steps to Achieving Personal and Organizational Greatness* by Palgrave Macmillan (2005). He lives in Ithaca, NY, and may be contacted at ccs7@cornell.edu or www.clintsidle.org